'A Killing a day': Supplying the British Army, 1793 to 1815

Dr. Chris Chilcott

Copyright © 2020 Chris Chilcott

All rights reserved.

ISBN: 9798677892936

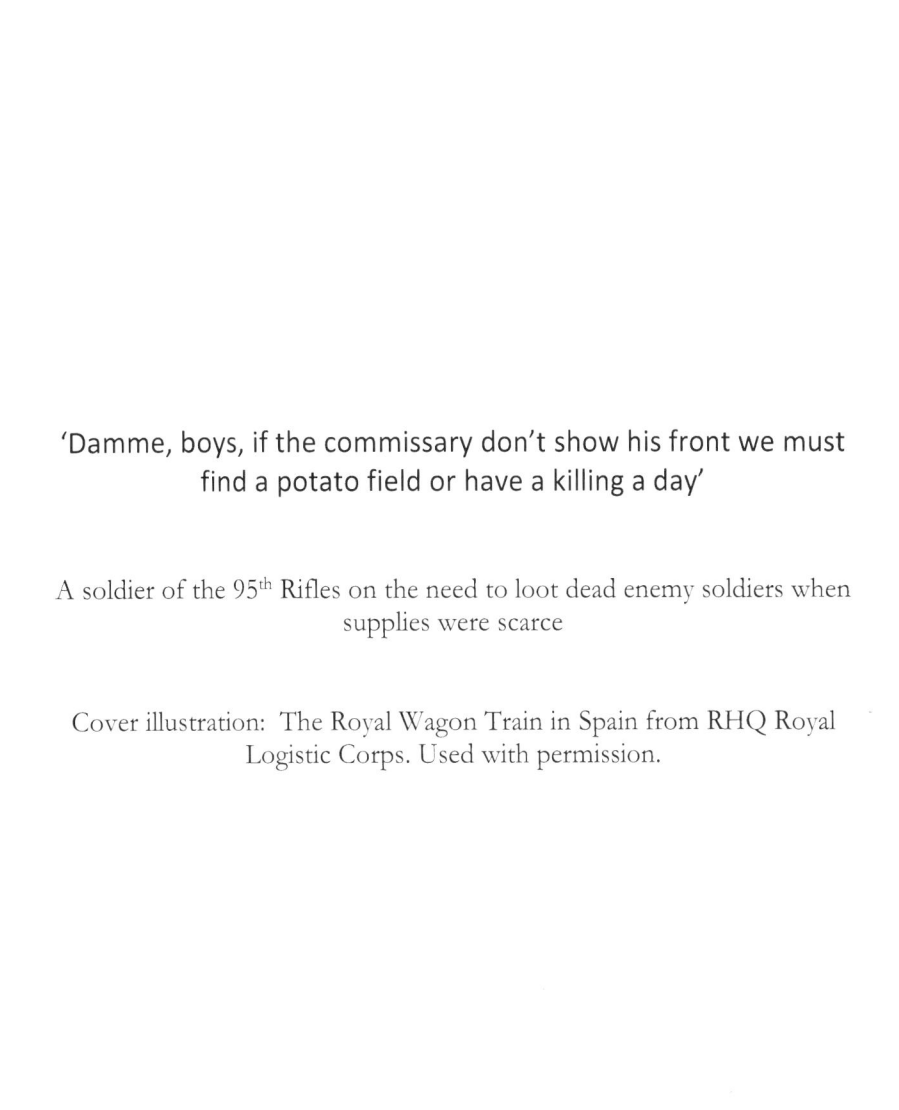

'Damme, boys, if the commissary don't show his front we must find a potato field or have a killing a day'

A soldier of the 95th Rifles on the need to loot dead enemy soldiers when supplies were scarce

Cover illustration: The Royal Wagon Train in Spain from RHQ Royal Logistic Corps. Used with permission.

CONTENTS

1	A system created from fear	5
2	The Treasury goes to war	24
3	Third in line	50
4	From A to B: Transport	78
5	A moral dimension	94
6	Counties versus Napoleon	126
7	Measuring success	144
8	Bibliography	148
9	Index of tables	153
10	Index	154

ACKNOWLEDGMENTS

My family and wife Natalie have not only sacrificed time and money but have well perfected that look of interest that serves to encourage a discussion and travels that they have little interest in! Several years ago the History Departments of the George Ward School and Bath Spa University led me down the academic history path that led to this work. There are the numerous friends and work colleagues who have encouraged me over the years and the members of Devizes & District Wargames Group, particularly Gareth Lowe and John Potter, who have been more than keen to engage in active discussion, and Phil Mackie for helping with the typography. Also my brother Rob who helped point me towards the publication path. Thanks to you all.

FORWARD

The initial intention of the foray into the British army of the Napoleonic Wars was to explore the experiences of soldiers from different cultures. The aim was to move away from hard data and explore experiences through the wealth of available letters, memories and diaries. What emerged was not so much a picture of differences but shared hardships. The evidence showed soldiers of many ranks and backgrounds were hungry, dressed in sometimes tattered uniforms. The question of 'why' was inevitable. This was the army of an industrialising power, arguably the wealthiest at the time, soon to possess one of the greatest Empires in history.

Once the question was asked the focus inevitably shifted to the hard data. The hardship experienced by soldiers was caused by lack of wagon movements and the tonnes of supplies delivered. Looking after soldiers also went beyond food and uniform, or even guns and tents. They required chaplains, medical services and education, and what of the wives and children who followed them even as they deployed overseas? This had implication for resources and strategy, and would form a keystone in plans to oppose a French invasion. How to maintain the army was a crucial question in the early nineteenth century, the problems however began with the creation of the modern army at the end of the seventeenth century.

CHAPTER 1

A system created from fear

The great misconception of the British army of the eighteenth and nineteenth century is that it achieved what it did because of the backing of the most industrially and economically advanced nation on the planet. In truth these achievements were made *despite* British economic and industrial policy. The illusion of a British army fully supported by industrializing Britain came about as the force appears to have enjoyed abundant success on the battlefield.

Initially dabbling on the peripheries of the European continent the army subsequently fought from Portugal, through Spain and into France. All this was whilst fighting colonial campaigns in Africa and Asia, alongside the War of 1812 against the United States. The result is a sanitized view of 'heroic' British achievements in the period 1793 to 1815. Nowhere is this more apparent than what is arguably the most famous battle of the era, the 1815 Battle of Waterloo. For fans of the Napoleonic British army the elephant in the room is that the battle, not even the last engagement of the wars, made little difference to the grand scheme of history. The best outcome Napoleon could have realistically hoped for was a bankrupt regime that limped on for a few more months before being swept away by a tide of

Austrians and Russians. As it was, the Prussians turned up on time giving Wellington the glory. Even European allies were swept along by the propaganda machine that went with Wellington, showering him with awards. Yet it was Empires of Russia and in particular Austria that kept bouncing back from defeat who consistently did the damage that sapped the strength of Napoleon's France. It was Russia that destroyed the French Grande Armée in 1812, not Wellington seeing off a few divisions in the Iberian Peninsula.

Ultimately Britain was no better or worse a military power on land than contemporary major powers and this was hardly surprising in the circumstances. The whole British establishment, military and civil, was recovering from the shock of losing the North American colonies. Whether this was due to the efforts of the colonists themselves or the interventions of Britain's continental rivals is a fair question. Neither was palatable to Britain at the end of the eighteenth century. Lack of prestige was further compounded by the consequences of a revolution closer to home – that in France. The British army found itself deployed in two roles to maintain the status quo, that of policeman at home and intervention force in Flanders. The later was a dismal failure and it was to be the best part of twenty years before the British army would again enjoy success on the continent. Within the British Isles the army was more successful, crushing the Irish Rebellion of 1798 with sometimes great brutality and suppressing civil disorder.

It is perhaps from the army's role in maintaining order in the British Isles that the less glorious aspects of its roles becomes clear. The blowing apart of French infantry formations has become acceptable, almost good sport, whilst these other roles have been allowed to be over looked or languish as footnotes. Certainly the idea of red coated infantry lining up to unleash a devastating volley at British subjects is uncomfortable. The role in policing and expanding the Empire even more so. As modern Britain wrestles with its colonial past it is significant that the army's excesses when policing the Empire are seen as a Victorian or later phenomenon but by the 1830s the pattern had already been set. It is as if the army that fought Napoleon was too busy for or even incapable of colonial atrocity. It is a misconception far from the truth.

Even when colonialism was less concerned with subduing indigenous peoples and more about stealing the colonies from other powers the British army's role is conveniently downplayed. These campaigns were little more than a land grab for rich commodities such as sugar in the Caribbean or to enlarge existing territories as in Africa. Such campaigns sit uneasily with the concept of a war waged to counter a revolution in France and feel more like opportunistic plunder. Even less comfortable is the link with slavery and the sacrifice of soldiers who died by the hundreds in disease ridden hospitals to keep the British flag flying in these Caribbean colonies. Little wonder that many historians of the British army in the period have contented themselves with a focus on the old enemy of France and the clearer cut war aims of the conflict on continental Europe.

Given that finance was the driving force behind much of Britain's policy in the era of the Napoleonic Wars it took historians a surprisingly long time (a little under 200 years in fact) to come up with a term for this - a 'fiscal-military state'. This was a form of state backed capitalism, in which the state sought to maximize profits. Many other aspects of the state developed because of the need to raise money. Taxation, for example, was not new but the British state had created by the end of the eighteenth century whole new systems and government departments to support this activity. The result was a growing civil services and the need to raise more taxes to support the state's tax raising activities. Slightly sinister for liberals of the day was that if the state raising finance was the goal, anything else – including 'liberty' and 'freedom' came second. This was a regime that attacked equality as an evil of the French Revolution; it was a system laying the foundations for the human rights abuses by industrialists that would shock Victorians out of their lethargy. For now, however, the abuses were at an acceptable level and there was the bogeyman of France against which to unite.

Morality and liberty aside, the existence of a fiscal-military state made Britain stronger. The reality of the situation for the army was that the force could not be allowed to fully benefit from nation's increasing strength. In the decades prior to 1800 Britain had experienced leaps in technology, improvements to infrastructure and massive financial benefits that no other country could replicate. Britain led the field in science, exploration and Imperial ambition. It possessed an Empire that would continue to expand at the expense of indigenous peoples across the globe.

Britain's achievements were made possible by a taxation and financial system unrivalled by any nation. This system could only continue if spending on the military – both land and naval - was contained. Higher taxes, disruption to markets and reductions in available labour were all dangers posed by a growing military to British prosperity. Technological advances in agriculture and industry only served to worsen the potential disruption. Mechanization made British labourers three times more productive than their European counterparts. This was great news for industrialists but every labourer that ended up in the armed forces also represented a far higher loss of production than it would otherwise have been. The result was a system of government and expenditure created with the intention of limiting the growth of the army.

The system was born in the aftermath of the disorder created by the English Civil War. This was an era of a failed republic, military dictatorship and restoration of monarchy. The army was heavily involved in all these events, creating a widespread mistrust of the force across the British Isles. The New Model Army that won the English Civil War for Parliament in 1648 rapidly proved that it wanted to dictate politics as much events on the battlefield. The army purged Parliament and supported Cromwell's seizure of power. With a brutality that would have impressed Stalin it systematically smashed opposition and stifled dissent across the realm. In Ireland and Scotland the force was particularly ruthless and counted prisoners, priests and children amongst its victims. Shocked by their own role in the brutal dictatorship and fearing a backlash from the populace, a faction of the army led by General Monck threw in its lot with the Stuart cause. It was by this stage far too late to save the reputation of the army. By supporting Cromwell it had made a deal with the devil.

One of the first actions of the restored Stuart government of 1660 was to look at ways of keeping the army out of politics. If this happy state of affairs had continued then perhaps all would have been forgotten but the restored Stuarts proved as inept as Cromwell was brutal. The era of the restored monarchy was marked by paranoid fears of creeping Catholicism in the House of Stuart, and all the murder and mayhem that would result from a Catholic sitting on the throne. That Catholics on the continent had long ceased burning Protestants at the stake had apparently gone unnoticed Britain. It was feared that a Catholic takeover would be achieved through the introduction of Irish Catholic troops into the English army by King James. The growing paranoia was to result in a foreign sponsored coup. In 1688 William III landed at Torbay leading to the so called Glorious Revolution.

The revolution of 1688 was allegedly Glorious due to its low body count. As ever, while fighting in England was limited, that in Scotland and Ireland was far from bloodless and included the Battle of the Boyne. The whole revolution could easily have gone in favour of James II had he held his nerve. As it was, prior to a probable engagement with William's forces near Salisbury James suffered a severe nosebleed and fled to France. The army had served James well at the Battle of Sedgemoor in 1685 when it had seen off another potential usurper - James' nephew the Duke of Monmouth – but now leaderless the force deserted en mass. Had James' nasal passage been more resilient the history of the British army and the British Isles itself may have been quite different. As it was William seized the crown and, he hoped, with it an army to fight the French.

The opportunistic William sought the English Crown as a means to an end rather than an ambition in its own right. Getting the troops, however, was not going to be easy. While desertion to his cause had been widespread following the flight of James, before this event it had been but a trickle of turn coats, mainly officers. More ominously if an army had deserted once it could do so again. Disloyal regiments were disbanded while others sent to fight in the Netherlands. While ridding William of potential opposition this did not significantly increase forces in the theatre as a number of regiments, English and Scottish, had travelled to England with William. Even worse was that William faced the prospect of James returning to reclaim his crown. The prize of the English crown had the potential to rapidly become a burden.

While pleased to see a good Protestant on the throne the English establishment had no desire to see a return to unrestricted large armies. Charles II had avoided the fate of his successor in part by maintaining only a small permanent force. Initially this had been a mere 6 regiments and a garrison in Tangier. James had expanded the army enough to alarm some but the financial burden had remained relatively small. It was the intended use of that army which caused alarm, not its size. England had become used to small armies and it has become somewhat embedded in defence policy ever since. With the exception of the two world wars the British army has consistently been kept small by cash conscious governments. Parliament found that in William they had a king who was more interested in troops than royal power, whilst he was both desperate and willing to listen. It was the resulting 1689 Bill of Rights that turned William's coup into a revolution.

In the Bill of Rights William mortgaged the ancient divine right of Kings to rule as they pleased in exchange for money and troops. The Bill established that a standing army required the consent of Parliament, formalizing a system in which the crown commanded the army but Parliament paid for its upkeep. This was not entirely new and Royal demands for Parliament to fund an army had been a point of contention for centuries, from 1689 this was enshrined in law. From this point the situation in England was unlike any other in Europe. Continental armies were the property of the crown, in the United Kingdom it would rapidly become a tool of Parliament. In 1699 the Disbanding Act went as far as establishing the number of troops that could be maintained. William had achieved his goal of extra troops to fight his enemies but this was increasingly on the terms of Parliament.

William's wars of the 1690s were funded through taxation, while the forces of the Duke of Marlborough that fought in the Wars of the Spanish Succession were paid for with credit. The national debt was born and the Bank of England created to support the nations finances. Overseeing this was a growing number of civil servants. The wave of new taxes used to finance the wars against Napoleon, from glass tax to excise duties, were administered by departments that had arisen to finance the wars of William III.

By the mid-eighteenth century the balance of power between crown and state in running the army had shifted significantly in the latter's favour. It was apparent that any political aspirations possessed by the army had long been tamed. There were occasional worries that individual troops may join in popular unrest. Such concerns reached a peak in the hysteria following the French Revolution but it was evident that there were never concerns about the army's ability to maintain order. This is not to say that small numbers of troops did not become disaffected (this was an era of revolution) but they were easily contained. The days of soldiers marching into Westminster had clearly passed. For Parliament this was a victory but one that brought with it the burden of paying for the army.

Taking control of the army had helped to create a financial system second to none. Taxation was regulated and helped fuel foreign policy supporting Imperialism, opening up markets that created wealth. The problem was that the British government found its military aspirations a prisoner of a system that prioritized generating revenue. A large army would have used resources seen by the beneficiaries of this as better spent on industrial expansion at home and imperial expansion overseas. The Royal Navy escaped as the fleet safeguarded both the home islands and mercantile interests. Its status was further enhanced by explorers such as Cook and Flinders, whose exploits further focused the nation's interest on naval matters. Spurred on by naval victories such Quiberon (1759), and glossing over fiascos such as the Medway (1667), Britain had by the nineteenth century gained a belief in her maritime destiny.

Grand strategy and geopolitics were all well and good but the preference for the fleet over the army in British society also existed for more practical reasons. The Royal Navy was militarism at arm's length. The wooden walls of the fleet kept the enemy out of gun range. So too did the personnel of the fleet remain well away, spending most of their time on ship rather than ashore. Throughout history this has proved to be either advantageous and disastrous for discipline. On the one hand sailors aboard ship are isolated from disorder and unrest ashore, on the other discord can spread rapidly amongst a ship's crew once it takes hold. For the citizens of Britain the relative detachment of sailors from the population was particularly beneficial. A sailor aboard ship could not cause trouble ashore but soldiers, maybe quartered in towns without barracks, were far more disruptive.

Alcohol fueled fights were a feature of life in garrison towns. Recruiting sergeants frequently plied potential recruits with drink and fueled this up to the very doors of the barracks. Existing rivalries were resolved with fists, whilst new rivalries were created. Recruits from Ireland were particularly prone to fights between Catholic and Protestants. Such disorder could be dangerous to inhabitants and on occasion required the deployment of other military forces to restore order until rowdy new recruits could be 'tamed' by military discipline. Such discipline generally contained the worst excesses but could breakdown spectacularly.

A particularly serious outbreak of disorder occurred amongst troops billeted in Cork during September 1795. Troops of the 105th and 113th Regiments of Foot, en route to the West Indies, mutinied, marching through the city with bayonets fixed and releasing prisoners from the jail. Needless to say the scenes caused considerable concern amongst the inhabitants of the city. Control was eventually restored relatively bloodlessly following the imposition of a curfew and arrival of troops from the 7th Dragoon Guards. This and similar events gave civilians ample reason for civilians to oppose the presence of soldiers in a locality. The use of the army to maintain control at times of public disorder further alienated sections of the population.[1]

By the outbreak of the Revolutionary War the army was necessary but citizens preferred it not to disrupt their lives. It could be disruptive at a local level but was perceived as a force that could be relied on to maintain order. The final decade of the eighteenth century was one characterized by fear of French revolutionary fervour reaching Britain. The Irish Rebellion of 1798 seemed to vindicate such fears. This was a time of agitation and ideas. Inevitably individual soldiers read seditious pamphlets, felt aggrieved or became involved in disorder, some deserted. It was however the Royal Navy that succumbed to a more general collapse of discipline that threatened the cohesion of the fleet. Widespread mutinies broke out in 1797 at Nore and Spithead. Here the isolation of sailors aboard ship had allowed disorder to spread.

The army brutally crushed the Irish Rebellion, deployed lethal force to suppress riots and sent units to deal with its own disaffected troops. This was a force confident of the loyalty of its rank and file. The government deployed troops to Northern England to suppress Luddite disturbances in 1812 (more troops in fact than sent to Spain in 1808), whilst troops were deployed in large numbers to the capital in 1815 to quell further disorder. One of Britain's premier heavy cavalry regiments, the Scots Greys, served on policing duties in England for much of the Napoleonic Wars, latterly being hacked down by French cavalry at Waterloo.

Clearly the army was loyal but ultimately to whom? In theory the monarch commanded the army due to the oath taken upon enlistment. In reality Royal influence had declined significantly since the reign of William III and the oath was ceremonial. The result was that by the time of Napoleon the army was a tool of parliament or, more specifically, whatever government was in power. Leading the government was the Prime Minister but the influence of this office over the army was limited due to the nature of British politics. The Prime Minister did not necessarily lead the largest political group in parliament, or even draw members of the government from his party. As a consequence the role of the Prime Minister was one of performing a political balancing act as much as formulating policy. Of the Prime Ministers in the early nineteenth century, only William Pitt (Prime minister 1783 to 1801 and again 1804 to 1806) and William Grenville (1806 to 1807) became seriously involved in the affairs of the army. Pitt was one of the instigators of the army's involvement in operations against enemy colonies and reformed the national command structure through creating the post of Secretary for War and the Colonies; Grenville's Foxite Ministry of Talents fell following attempts to reform the army.

The principal means through which a Prime Minister was

able to influence the actions and structure of the army was through the appointment of his Cabinet. Although attempts were made to run the affairs of government through consensus the personality of those individuals appointed to lead ministries and departments could be significant. Of particular importance to the army were: the Foreign Office, the policies of which could dictate where and when the army was deployed; the Home Office, which had jurisdiction over militia, fencible and volunteer forces, and the Treasury. The latter was possibly one of the largest and most important government departments and, amongst other roles, was responsible for the Commissariat. This was the principal organization tasked with supplying the force. Two Cabinet posts had more direct control of the army. These were the Master General of the Ordnance and the Secretary of State for War and the Colonies. The former was head of the Ordnance Board, which had responsibility for the engineers and artillery, but had only an advisory role in Cabinet. Conversely, the Secretary of State for War and the Colonies was a government post and had more influence over policy.

Despite the powers over the army granted to it Parliament, through the Cabinet and then the Secretary of War, could do little more than order the army into a theatre of war and issue guidance, such as on the need to avoid casualties or to aid an allied nation. On occasion politicians did intervene more directly but in such circumstances the army rarely met with success. In 1809 political concerns resulted in the ill-fated Walcheren Expedition. Austria was yet again at war with France and as ever facing defeat. Instead of expanding the British commitment in Spain and Portugal, the British opted to land an army in a disease infested swamp. Inevitably massive casualties followed despite little enemy action.

Walcheren demonstrated a lack of strategic understanding on the part of politicians. The army, however, could not be trusted to act entirely without guidance. This was demonstrated by the ineptly executed Buenos Aires expedition of 1806. This was a military disaster that resulted in the humiliating surrender of the British expeditionary force to local militia and had far reaching political repercussions. The event gave the Spanish colonists a new self-belief and increased their determination to achieve independence from Spanish colonial rule. This was an event British foreign policy makers sought to avoid or delay for as long as possible. The result was a chain of events leading to revolution in South America and ultimately the creation of the Monroe doctrine in the USA. This would drive major events in the twentieth century as the United States believed it was its right to police the America's. If the army had asked for political guidance in 1806 the world today would be a different place.

Below the Secretary of State for War and the Colonies the national command structure of the army became more complex. The combat elements of the army were divided between those of Horse Guards (regular infantry and cavalry), the Ordnance Board (regular artillery and engineers) and the Home Office (militia, yeomanry, fencibles and volunteers). It is apparent that there was no single military department with responsibility for the entire army. Of the three departments only Horse Guards had a soldier in charge, known as the Commander-in-Chief. The control exercised by the Home Office over auxiliary forces was only nominal with the result that the British army was effectively divided into two departments. It is inexplicable how no major clashes of jurisdiction were to occur in the period although inefficiency was inevitable.

The office of Commander-in-Chief for much of the Revolutionary and Napoleonic Wars was held by Frederick, Duke of York, George III's second son. York temporarily left office in 1809 following a dalliance with a lady by the name of Mary Clark. Cleared by Parliament of any wrongdoing, York resigned as a matter of honor. York returned in 1811 but the interim Commander-in-Chief General David Dundas had merely continued York's policies, having too little time to do much damage. That York held the post of Commander-in-Chief almost continually from 1796 to 1827 would suggest a stagnant and conservative administration.

As a field commander York's performance was so bad that that he was immortalized in a child's nursery rhyme entitled 'The Grand Old duke of York'. Fortunately for the army York was unafraid of innovation and a first class administrator. Reforms implemented during his time in office included regimental schools, a staff college, published rules and regulations for non-commissioned officers and a subsidized mail service. Such reforms helped drag the army from its nadir of the previous decade and directly improved morale. Besides the infantry and cavalry, Horse Guards contained two departments. These were the Quartermaster General, who was responsible for troop movements, information gathering and the supply of camping equipment, and the Adjutant-General, who was responsible for drill and discipline.

The combat arms not under Horse Guards – the artillery and engineers – were the responsibility of the Ordnance Board. The two organizations had developed along markedly different lines. Horse Guards had at its head a soldier and, until 1811, a civilian secretary, the situation in the Ordnance was reversed. The head of the Ordnance was a civilian with a seat in the Cabinet but below him was an army officer, known as the Deputy Adjutant General. The Deputy Adjutant General's department was created to rectify a peculiarity of the Royal Artillery - specifically that despite being granted the title of 'regiment' it lacked many of the administrative organs associated with such a formation. Prior to the creation of the department it had been the responsibility of the individual company and battalion officers deployed around the globe to transmit inspection returns to the Ordnance Board and make requests concerning supplies.

The Ordnance Board had existed for centuries and was very much a product of previous eras, with implications for its structure and efficiency. Although the role of the Ordnance had changed over the centuries it continued to have at its head the Master General of the Ordnance, a post perceived as being one of the most important and prestigious in the United Kingdom. Its responsibilities included supplying the Royal Navy and army with munitions, although it was the latter that virtually monopolized the board's time. It was common for the Masters General to hold other posts and they were frequently active in the House of Lords. Unfortunately for the Ordnance the activities of the Masters General tended to focus not on their duties butt rather their own careers and interests.

---

[1] John Travers to Lord Lismore, Cork, 4th September 1795, NAM 6807/370/43 to 44.

CHAPTER 2

The Treasury goes to war

As the British army entered the nineteenth century its logistics was a tangle of departments. The Quarter Master General distributed camping equipment, entrenching tools and slack lime to dispose of animal carcasses. The Store Master General kept accounts of goods in depots and packed stores, while the Ordnance seemed to content to do its own thing and had its own organisations. Of all the various departments, the most important organisation in terms of reach and capability was the Commissariat.

It is fair to say that the Commissariat had something of an identity crisis. It's personnel travelled with the army in war zones but were civilians. Addressed as mister they wore blue uniforms. The organisation had arisen to prominence in the seventeenth century, when Charles II appointed the Commissary General to oversee pay and muster records. Along the way it had gained a variety of responsibilities and by 1800 had become the most important organisation within the logistics system. The Commissariat continued to absorb the roles of other departments and in 1810 took over the supply of forage from the Quarter Master General.

When a British army arrived overseas one of the first tasks of the Commissariat would be to roam the country for supplies and sites for depots. The importance of this activity was such that it featured in strategic planning and diplomats were assigned to travel with the commissaries. Upon arriving in Spain in 1808 General Sir John Moore was directed by the government to liaise with the Commissary General to determine 'the best means of assembling an adequate supply of horses and mules for rendering your army mobile'. At the same time a group of agents was travelling to Asturias to procure 'such horses and mules as that country can furnish'.[2]

It was all well and good to give Moore a point of contact, somewhat concerning however was that his force had been deployed to Spain without the means to make it 'mobile'. Clearly Moore would have to make do with what he could get. There was an over confidence in the ability of British cash to solve the problem, a confidence that proved to be unfounded. Not only were the animals acquired in too small numbers, with artillery pieces left immobile, but cash was not limitless. The wealth of Britain was only any good in the hands of purchasing agents. The result was that at both home and abroad payments were often made with promissory notes. Inevitably suppliers and particularly those overseas were less than enthusiastic about such payments.[3]

Goods were commonly stored in depots overseen by Commissariat storekeepers. Depots could be separated by many miles, or concentrated in small areas, depending on the items stored in them and the requirements of the locality concerned. In Dublin there existed four depots located at various buildings, all of which were rented by the Commissariat. During 1806 it was decided to investigate the possibility of relocating the four Dublin depots to a single, specially constructed building. This was to cost £6,713 for five storeys but it was discovered that if reduced to four storeys the cost would amount to only £5,609. Besides saving £831 paid for rent each year, the single depot would require only one assistant storekeeper rather than the four then employed. This represented a total saving (in rent and wages) of £1037 17s per annum. The scheme proved successful and the policy of amalgamating depots was implemented across Ireland. By 1811, of the sixteen towns and cities in which Commissariat depots were located, only one, Enniskillen, was listed as having two.[4]

It would be easy to say that the amalgamations in Ireland showed the Commissariat was striving for efficiency. The reality was that such inefficiencies had been allowed to develop. They may well have continued was it not parliamentary scrutiny of spending which only increased as the military budget expanded. During the eighteenth-century, the Committee for Public Accounts ensured that expenditure remained under examination, while detailed investigations were conducted for Reports of Military Enquiry.

While at a depot the primary role of Commissariat personnel was ensuring the distribution of supplies, monitoring stock levels and keeping accounts. There may be a perception of Commissariat being staffed by quill pen wielding accountants. While this has some truth (see below) depots would have been the center of various activities. Branding irons and stamps were employed by storekeepers to identify Commissariat property and various weights and measures were also utilized. A typical Commissariat store contained scales and weights for candles ranging from ten ounces to eight pounds and coal measures in quarter, half and whole bushels.

Commissaries were authorized to sell items that were damaged and judged too costly to repair or simply no longer required. Items often included include camping equipment but also ammunition pouches and bayonet holders. That the latter items were sold to civilians is surprising in an era when the government seemed to fear its populace as much as its foreign enemies. Other items that could be sold included unwanted mules and horses, along with the offal and hides of cattle slaughtered while on campaign. Soldiers were also required to pay through deductions of pay for lost or damaged uniforms and equipment. The sums of money involved could be considerable and from 1810 cavalrymen were expected to pay 7s 6½d for new water decks and 4s 2d for corn sacks.[5]

The storage of specific items required special consideration. Extensive cold stores were not utilized for meat as livestock would be slaughtered as required or meat preserved by salting, smoking or similar methods. The storage of fodder was complex and caused difficulties: old straw could not be mixed with new but new and old hay could be mixed freely. The differences were lost on some Commissariat staff and forage ruined. Barrels were a common type of storage vessel used for certain liquids, fodder, food and gunpowder. Several Commissariat stations – including Heligoland and New South Wales - employed coopers permanently, while others – such as Malta and Sicily - employed them on a semi-permanent basis. Much effort went into the storage of bread, with two types of vessel were employed for this purpose. In the field a wooden basket was used, while in Commissariat stores and a more robust version braced by iron was standard. The Commissariat took such matters seriously and an individual caught issuing the wrong type of bread basket could receive a severe reprimand.[6]

Despite the threat of disciplinary action over bread baskets, the chests that stored the cash were the most important storage vessel for the Commissariat. Money was the life blood of the organization. Stations such as those in Sicily held a variety of currencies, in that case pounds sterling and both Spanish and Sicilian dollars. There existed no fewer than 34 coded accounting categories to manage the sometimes considerable sums of money for which Commissariat personnel could be responsible. This included money held in pay chests for both goods and services.[7]

Categories	
Imprests	Commissariat contingencies
Bat & forage	Medical department
Staff pay	Deputy paymaster general
Military contingencies	Portuguese government
Secret service	Spanish government
Clothing & field equipment	Loss on bills negotiated
Ordnance department	Property Tax
Engineering department	Pay of Commissariat department
Supplies	Treasury Bills
Purchase of horses mules etc	Sums received from accountants
Labourers	Stores & provisions sold by authority
Transport by land	Property tax charged upon incomes
Transport by water	Bills from the Ordnance commissary & paymaster
Indemnifications	Sums received, no particular abstract allocated
Prisoners of war	Balances paid
Stationery & printing	Bills received upon paymaster in England

Figure 1: Commissariat accounting categories.

Commissariat personnel were responsible for considerable sums of money that were either held in pay chests or used to pay for goods and services. It was a system open to fraud that sometimes lacked even basic precautions. Until the Napoleonic Wars it was even the case that receipts were not always required to claim costs for purchases. It was a naïve level of trust to put in the hands of personnel and fraud caused irreparable damage to the Commissariat's reputation. Corruption was very much a part of life in the period, and that the Commissariat's personnel were from professions such as accountants amongst whom integrity varied. Aided by a push supplies 'fell' from wagons at convenient times, the pay of deserted muleteers was claimed and expenses drawn for unissued cheques. Educated commissariat personnel were also able to take advantage of illiterate soldiers and civilians, often paying out promissory notes at half value. Such was the nature of record keeping at the time it is difficult to judge the cost of fraud to the Commissariat. Items were not tracked from procurement to distribution. There may have a been a torrent of equipment and cash leaving stores illegally, equally there may have been a trickle (more likely somewhere between the two). Whatever the case it was at a sufficient level for the Commissariat to act.

The response to fraud was increasing regulation directed primarily at those responsible for stores. Instructions included requirements for receipts, a second signature on bills and monthly reports. That the organization remained solvent without such measures is testament to the integrity of most personnel. Reforms continued and shortfalls in the delivery of supplies to units, whether due to shortages in the depot or their not being required, were to be regularly reported to prevent them being sold on illegally. Additional instructions, issued in July 1815, prevented commissaries claiming funds on behalf of other departments, such as the artillery and engineers. Furthermore equipment could only be removed from stores with the permission of designated personnel, rank alone being insufficient to authorize the removal of stores.

To reduce fraud accounts were carefully controlled and administered. The result was an increasingly bureaucratic with 23 separate articles, requiring seven different forms that governed expenditure on forage for cavalry units in Ireland. By the end of the era paperwork threatened to surpass logistics as the primary aim of the organization. In 1811 a Commissary Hagan incorrectly listed shirts after shoes in a list of expenses and received a reprimand more severe than that given by a fellow commissary known to have 'misplaced' militia stores (including ordnance) in potentially rebellious Ireland! Increasing bureaucracy led to the Commissariat being split into two branches, designated stores and accounts. The latter became so large that by 1816 half of the organization's personnel in garrisons could be employed in accounts.[8]

Even before the reforms of the 1810s, the most important elements in Commissariat bureaucracy were the ledgers and account books. Commissariat accountants were issued four ledgers and instructed to carry them at all times, 'on every march and change of station'. Each ledger was colour coded according to its intended use – brown for income and expenditures, green for provisions, blue for transfers of stores and red for provisions issued to troops.

Day of month	Return to be received
1	Pay estimates
11	Abstracts of bills to Portuguese
15	Costs of hired vessels
24	Monthly cash and store accounts
25	Provisions supplied to regiments Abstract of bills to the Spanish Forage, Shortfalls in deliveries

Schedule of Commissariat returns.[9]

Returns were to reach the Commissary General by a given day of each month or week. In an era more commonly associated with Emperors and dashing cavalry charges, we find the requests for weekly returns to arrive by Monday morning or in some cases Thursday. Serviceable and unserviceable items were only distinguished in the monthly, rather than weekly, returns. The regular monitoring of accounts limited the damage done by both fraud and incompetence. During the winter of 1810, for example, it was noted that although no deceit was involved certain regiments were still waiting to pay for uniforms six months after being issued them. Incompetence was most often addressed through written warnings, reprimands or dismissal.[10]

Improvements in administrative efficiency were one thing, translating this to operations were another. Transportation was a bottleneck in the system that was never fully overcome. Ironically administrative efficiency elevated the problem by the need to have wagons allocated to transport the ledgers! The two elements of difficulty for transport were the draught animals and wagons they hauled. During the Peninsula War the army used a veritable menagerie of horses, mules and oxen to haul its wagons. There was never enough to go around and in 1811, it was proposed that the Royal Artillery acquire mules from the Commissariat to transport mobile forges. The plan was never implemented, maybe due to the realization that said forges needed supplies delivered by Commissariat wagons.[11]

Britain boasted a good road network for the period but beyond the port of embarkation had little value to the army. Spain and Portugal in particular were noted for their poor roads. In Spain there existed Royal Roads, constructed using the latest building techniques and 30 to 60 feet wide but these were few in number, linked only major cities and were badly maintained. The most common types of roads were caminos and carrils. Caminos were dirt tracks while the carrils had two rows of paving stones that only in theory eased the passage of wheeled vehicles. Accidents were common and the roads soon became congested by heavy traffic. While accompanying a wagon train to Almeida during the winter of 1812, Conductor of Stores W. Morris recorded in his diary that 'we could scarcely make any way in consequence of the road being crowded with bullock cars conveying the sick and wounded baggage'. Added to Morris' problems was that four days later the column did not move at all because they were still awaiting orders concerning the route that they were to take.[12]

The sometimes chaotic allocation of personnel further hindered Commissariat transport. This was apparent in 1808 when elements of the army were deployed for action in Spain. Lieutenant-General Sir David Baird was instructed to lead to the country a sizeable contingent of reinforcements that consisted of seven infantry battalions and two companies of artillery. The force was to travel from Cork to Falmouth but was delayed for three weeks by the late arrival of transport vessels. Eventually arriving in Falmouth and already several weeks late, Baird discovered that several key personnel were not awaiting his arrival. This was reported to the War Office, the general informing the Secretary for War that 'I think it necessary to appraise your Lordship also that I have not as yet heard of any paymaster or commissary being appointed to this army'. Two days later a commissary reported for duty. Baird promptly informed the War Office that he would take matters into his own hands by appropriating further personnel if the situation was not resolved. The force eventually left Falmouth on 9 October, over a month late but with its full complement of Commissariat personnel.[13]

The Napoleonic Wars were a global war and perhaps deserved the title of a World War. This influenced the deployment of the Commissariat and in turn its efficiency due to the need to maintain stores and distribute supplies in far flung our posts. The overseas deployments of the Commissariat in December 1816 are summarized in figure 3. Remarkably there existed standardized forms for returns, expenses and requisition but no consistent terminology for the regions in which the army operated. Hence the terms cited are the those in one particular Commissariat document.

Region	Location	Personnel
Africa	Cape Colony	30
	Mauritius	24
	Africa	15
	Total	69
Caribbean	Bahamas	5
	Bermuda	12
	Honduras	2
	West Indies	10
	Windward & Leeward Islands	98
	Total	127
Europe	France	150
	Portugal	79
	Gibraltar	21
	United Kingdom	52
	Mediterranean	97
	Heligoland	3
	Total	402
North America	Canada	137
	Newfoundland	16
	Nova Scotia	46
	Total	199
Australia	New South Wales	44
Grand total		**841**

Figure 3: The Global Deployment of the Commissariat, December 1816.[14]

Evidently the British managed to rule an Empire without telling administrators what to call all of its regions. West Africa, Goree and Africa were frequently used interchangeably. In this data the stations in Malta, Sicily and the Ionian Islands were all included under a single heading of the Mediterranean, while in other cases cited individually. Of note is the absence of Commissariat personnel in regions such as the Indian subcontinent, a region that was the responsibility of the East India Company.

An impact of administrative reforms resulted in some regions having distinct stores and accounts departments. Figure 4 illustrates how personnel were divided between stores and accounts in a number regions that had both such departments.

Posting	Personnel employed in:	
	Accounts	Stores
Canada	125	12
Cape Good Hope	26	4
Gibraltar	11	10
Mauritius	18	6
Mediterranean	85	12
Nova Scotia	41	5
Portugal	60	19

Fig 4: Commissariat stores and accounts, December 1816.

The data hides a considerable number of bureaucrats as administration was not solely the domain of the accounts department. Stores departments themselves employed a considerable number of administrators. Of the 125 personnel employed in stores in Canada, fifty-three were clerks supported by two office runners. This gave Canada a total of 62 out of 125 staff being employed as administrators. In Britain the manpower of the Commissariat at this point appears to have been almost entirely administrative and among its fifty-two personnel there were four chief clerks, thirty-eight clerks, three messengers and one office keeper. After two decades of war the organization had evolved from storekeeping to book keeping.

There was no typical Commissariat station and personnel were employed to fulfil a wide range of tasks depending on local requirements. In Bermuda and Malta boatmen were employed and the Commissariat in New South Wales had a bookbinder on its strength. Nova Scotia was the only station to record the specific roles of its issuers (either fuel or food) and in 1816 Mauritius was the sole location in which a store serjeant (sic.) was present. In Calais in February 1816 there was a small commissariat station, consisting of a deputy commissary, an assistant deputy, two clerks and two store keepers. During 1816 the senior Commissariat officers in France (with 150 personnel), Portugal (with 79) and Canada (with 137) were Commissaries General. Although larger than the department in Portugal, that in the Windward and Leeward Islands, along with the Mediterranean, were split between several locations and in consequence three Assistant Commissary Generals region shared command. In Honduras the senior Commissariat officer was only a temporary clerk, the affairs of the department being overseen by a committee that was collectively granted the rank of Deputy Assistant Commissary General.

The Commissariat was a cosmopolitan organization. This was hardly surprising when it is considered that the ranks of the British army in the period included Irish, Scots, Welsh, English, Poles, Germans, Spaniards, Portuguese and French emigres. In Sicily in 1813 Commissariat personnel comprised eight 'Italians', five Sicilians, four English and one Swiss. Many Germans served as Commissaries in Europe but possibly the most important overseas personnel of the Commissariat were those Spanish and Portuguese employed as muleteers to transport supplies during the Peninsula War.[15]

A column of wagons led by muleteers was no doubt a welcome sight for many soldiers as it could mean new supplies of food. This is the commodity that is most associated with the Commissariat and its supply had highly visible failings. The subject of food is broad and includes not only biscuit, meat and bread but also drinking water, alcohol and fodder. If the Commissariat failed to ensure adequate supplies of food troops would be required to spend more time foraging, while generals could not plan future operations with any certainty. In the worst case scenario an army deprived of food may collapse into a starving rabble, looting friend and foe alike in an effort to survive. British soldiers were particularly vulnerable to this and fell apart faster than the French at times of shortage.

An insight into the type and quantity of food supplied by the army to its troops can be gained from a return of the supplies available to the army in December 1813. Those available to three infantry divisions are shown in figure 5:

Division	Days supplies of		
	Bread & biscuit	Meat	Wine & spirits
3rd	5	13	2
4th	1	13	2
7th	None	11	3

Figure 5: Availability of supplies in the center army corps, December 1813.[16]

Despite occupying an approximately similar geographical position in the same time frame, the level of supply to the three divisions was inconsistent. The 3rd division possessed only two days of full supply and the 4th one, while the 7th did not have sufficient quantities of every element for a single day. Alcohol in all three was in limited supply.

There was a significant disparity between reserves of meat when compared to that of bread and biscuit. This situation was due to the differences in how each was provided. Meat marched on the hoof with the army, was available regardless of season and could be slaughtered as required on the spot. Conversely bread and biscuits required some effort to produce and their manufacture was a relatively long process. Baking required the availability of wheat, which was not always available and also required processing. Another difficulty was procuring or manufacturing sufficient yeast. Great efforts were made by army bakers throughout the period to increase both the quality and cost effectiveness of this important ingredient. Finally, even if these difficulties could be overcome the baking of bread was time consuming. This to have an impact on strategy and planning at the highest levels.

During the Peninsular War providing grain proved to be particularly problematic due to the scarcity of that commodity in the theatre. Due to French domination of Europe this could only be rectified by importing great quantities directly from the United States, Canada and Brazil. Of the difficulties encountered regarding the supply of grain to the Peninsular army Arthur Wellesley noted that:

in the present season of the year [summer] you cannot depend upon the country for bread. Portugal never fed itself during more than seven months out of twelve, the common consumption of the country is Indian corn; and the little wheat there is in the country cannot be ground at this season of the year as the mills are generally turned by water and there is now no water in the mill ponds.[17]

Wellesley's comments not only highlighted the difficulties of procuring sufficient supplies but also the difficulties that could be encountered when milling. Added to these problems was the difficulty of transporting the required items, whether in raw (such as harvested crops) or refined (such as flour) forms.

Biscuit was a standby ration for when bread was not available. Easily stored and preserved it was useful for an army on the march but far less popular with soldiers. Regular stops to bake bread would have hindered an army on the march but there was no such difficulty when encamped. In consequence, units of hungry soldiers on occasion produced bread independently of the Commissariat, thrashing corn and grinding flour to bake bread on their own initiative. Such a situation arose following the Battle of Talavera in 1809. In that year stores of flour in Lisbon were so full that vessels allocated to transport it were reassigned to other tasks. Yet in the field soldiers went hungry as flour was not available to bake bread or biscuit. It says much for the backgrounds of British soldiers that units were able to find in their ranks soldiers able to harvest and mill flour before baking bread.[18]

The food supplied by the Commissariat was sometimes of questionable quality. In his melancholy 'Subaltern's Elergy' Ensign Meade complained of camp kettles 'yielding soup meagre to frighten swine'. Even those far from the fighting were not immune. Judge Advocate Larpent, based at army headquarters, complained that ration beef 'cooked up like Indian rubber', while a letter written concerning the Commissariat depot in Longford described a sample of biscuits containing 'dust and dirt and bad bits'. Severe shortages were also common. As the army marched through the Pyrenees in 1813 Rifleman Costello of the 95th Rifles stated that his daily ration consisted of a single biscuit per day, while Private Howell of 71st Regiment of Foot confessed to stealing the dog biscuits that he was preparing for the Duke of Wellington's hounds to relieve his hunger. That the Duke's hounds were better fed than common soldiers is a particularly damning indictment of the supply system and army in general.[19]

How did the Commissariat get things so wrong? Many of the difficulties were beyond the control of the organization but this merely passes blame onto the army more generally. Certainly there was unfairness in the system. Wellington's hounds ate while soldiers starved and the chewy beef served at headquarters was better than the empty camp kettles experienced in the field. That these camp kettles were empty suggests a visible failure of the Commissariat. However, even the best efforts of the Commissariat could be thwarted and soldiers went hungry despite the availability of food.

Meat was relatively easy to supply as it travelled with the army and could be easily be supplemented by hunting or poaching (the difference being one of ownership). Cooking the meat ration was often challenging, due to either a shortage of cooking implements or lack of time caused by rapid marches. The problem of scarce cooking implements was partly rectified following the widespread issue of tents later in the war. Mules were assigned to transport these while cooking utensils were carried by the men and thus available as soon as the unit encamped. This did not always ensure the safe and timely arrival of the required equipment. Troops carrying utensils could get delayed, redirected or even lost. Due to these risks, units tasked to carry items such as camp kettles received an armed escort. Initially such escorts were mounted dragoons but latterly soldiers on foot. No matter what escort was provided, utensils could only arrive if they had been issued. Although supplied with an adequate number of camp kettles in 1815 (157 – approximately one per four men), the 1st battalion of the 88th had an insufficient number of 'billy hooks' (94) to support them over fires. In 1809 the ratios had been even worse, at one kettle per 6 men and one hook per 10 men.[20]

As problematic as feeding the troops was sustaining the horses of the army. This was not merely a problem in regard to cavalry. The number of animals used by the infantry divisions should not be underestimated. In the 7th Infantry Division, serving in Spain in 1813 and consisting of 5,876 men, there were 244 horses, 268 mules operated by the regiments and 246 mules operated by the Commissariat, giving a total of 758 animals, which was the equivalent to a full-strength cavalry regiment. Added to the animals already consuming forage could be those that were not officially on the strength of the regiment or even in the army. General Cole maintained a menagerie consisting of ten goats, a cow and thirty-six sheep to supplement his rations. Even if the animals did not consume army fodder, their grazing would have consumed local supplies that could potentially have been utilized by the army. How they slowed the redeployment of headquarters can only be imagined.[21]

For units stationed in Britain a common difficulty relating to the maintenance of animals was not a shortage of fodder so much as an excess of this commodity. The seasonal production of forage inevitably resulted in gluts at certain times of year, with result that forage simply rotted. Forces in Spain and Portugal faced the opposite problem to those in Britain, and the difficulty was procuring sufficient fodder to begin with. In 1809 the cavalry ration was defined as being 14lb of hay, 12lb of oats or 10lb of barley per horse, while that of mules employed on supply operations was 30lbs corn per week. Demand could in part be met by importing forage from Britain, with 4.5 million pounds of straw and oats being requested in 1809. Other than this the Commissariat had little choice except to make do with what it could find in each region. On occasion commissaries resorted to issuing potentially harmful green corn and the depletion of fodder had implications for the local economy. This created a demand for fodder from locals, which Cavalrymen exploited by swapping their forage ration with locals for alcohol![22]

The market for fodder in return for alcohol was an example of the failing that characterized the Commissariat. There was little long term planning, of either demand or sustainability. The copious reams of paperwork in its ledgers and forms were about what had happened, sometimes the here and now but rarely about the future. The doctrine was fundamentally a reflexive one that reacted to situations rather than prepare for them. To be effective a logistics system requires an exact definition of requirements. This was lacking in the Commissariat's doctrine.

The first personnel from the organization to arrive in a region were purchasing agents. Their task was not one of establishing the ability of a province to sustain a force in the long term but rather to purchase what supplies it could for when the army arrived. This was to be achieved regardless of long-term consequences for the local economy. This impacted future procurement activities but depleting markets and increasing prices. Captain Bragge of the 3rd Dragoons noted of the vicinity of Belem in 1811 that 'the English have ruined this market as they do all others, and at this moment everything from a hens egg to a mule is dearer than in England'. Meanwhile Judge Advocate Larpent complained in May 1813 that 'we cannot buy anything to eat except honey, sugar, bacon, bread and cheese'. That Larpent was able to complain of only having food that hungry troops in the field would call luxuries says much about equality but the point is clear. If Larpent struggled to find supplies, so too would locals.[23]

The depletion of markets alone was not sufficient to end the activities of the Commissariat in a region. its personnel utilized many means to acquire supplies including tactics that could literally be those of an occupying army. To counter local attempts to conceal stores underground, commissaries resorted to the French practice of pouring water on the ground to locate areas of recently disturbed soil (where it drained away quicker). Some of the other methods used by commissaries were little more than terrorism and in 1813 a Commissary was found guilty of burning down a Spanish house. Commissaries also co-operated with guerrillas who themselves mistreated locals.[24]

The plundering of supplies was dramatically at odds with the concept that the army should cause as little disruption to civilians as possible. This was primarily a domestic policy but it was also in British interests not to alienate the populations of allies. There was also the need to be seen as liberators not invaders when advance into formerly French controlled territories. Ultimately, however, operational requirements would take precedence over political expediency and the practices normally utilized to placate civilians were ignored. Thus the Commissariat continued to utilize all means at its disposal when the situation warranted.

The ruthlessness of commissaries in the field was to have implications for the organization. In a country already devastated by war it was inevitable that the inhabitants of towns and villages would react with hostility to the arrival of a commissary intent on plundering what remained of local stocks. On occasion this led to violence and in 1810 Spanish civilians set upon two members of a foraging party, one receiving seven gunshot wounds and the other being shot through the lung. This was a consequence of a policy that sought to provide supplies through legalized plunder. It was a policy that did not maximize the potential of a region to sustain a force and could provide only a short-term solution to the problem of maintaining the army.[25]

[2] To Lieutenant-General Sir John Moore, Downing Street, 26th September 1808, PRO WO 1/236, War Department in Letters: Sir John Moore and General Baird, September 1808 to January 1809, p.9.
[3] Wellesley to Castlereagh, 8th August 1808, PRO WO 1/228.
[4] Elliot to Handfield, Dublin Castle, 27th July 1806, PRO WO 63/88-91, Entry Book of Letters Received at Commissariat Headquarters, Dublin, 1805 – 1812.
[5] *Letter from Barrak* [sic] *Master General to Barrak Masters* (Barracks Office, 1797); Major B. Woodward to Major Ramsey, Royal Barracks, 17th September 1810, PRO WO 63/91, p.148; General Order No. 188, PRO WO 63/91, p.49.
[6] N. Malissis to Mr. Dunne, Commissary General's Office, 12th January 1810, PRO WO 63/40-49
[7] Account Book of Assistant Commissary General George Grellier Statement of Money Remaining in the Military Chest, 1st January 1814, NAM 7902/36.
[8] June 1808, PRO T1/1061, Instructions to His Majesty's Deputy Commissary of Accounts; Commissary General to Mr Hagan, Cork, 17th April 1811, PRO WO 63/46; H. Webb to J. Jones, Commissary General's Office, 23rd February 1811, PRO WO 63/45
[9] NAM 6807-221, passim.
[10] 16th January 1811, NAM 6807/221, p.1.
[11] PRO WO 37/10/26, Papers Relating to Provision of Portable Forges, 1810-12, paragraph 17.
[12] NAM 7508/24, Notebook of W. Morris, Conductor of Stores, 1812.
[13] Lieutenant-General Baird, to Castlereagh, Falmouth, October 1808; Sir John Moore and General Baird, September 1808 to January 1809, PRO WO 1/236, Baird's force would face further delays due to lack of shipping and chaotic Spanish organization before disembarking in Galicia.
[14] PRO WO 61/25, Commissariat Department 1816 – 17.
[15] Monthly returns of those employed in the Commissariat Department under the control of Assistant Commissary General Grellier at Milazzo, 25th October 1813 to 24th November 1813, NAM 7902/36. Designation of nationality is drawn from the original source.
[16] NAM 7512/124, Supplies to the Divisions of the Centre Army Corps in the Peninsula, December 1813.
[17] Wellesley to Burrard, Aeyria, 11th August 1808, PRO WO 1/228, p.191.
[18] Bingham to mother, Delatosa, 10th August 1809, Vol. 1, NAM 6807/163, Bingham Letters, p.62.
[19] NAM 7505/10, J. R. Meade, 'The Subaltern's Elegy' (Spain, 1st July 1813); G. Larpent (ed), *The Private Journal of F S Larpent: Judge Advocate General of British Forces in the Peninsula*, 3 volumes, (London, Richard Bentley, 1853), Vol. 1, p.36; A. Brett-James (ed), *Edward Costello: The Peninsular and Waterloo Campaigns* (London, Longmans, 1967), p.122; C. Hibbert (ed), *A Soldier of the 71st* (London, Leo Cooper, 1976), pp.72-73.
[20] NAM 6112/689, Field Equipment Return for the 1st Battalion 88th Foot, 9th

June 1815.
[21] NAM 7512/124, December 1813; G. Larpent (ed), *The Private Journal of F S Larpent,* Vol 2, (London, Richard Bentley, 1853), p.65.
[22] Arthur Wellesley to Castlereagh, 31st May 1809, PRO WO 1/238; Standing Orders, Order No. 37, NAM 6807/221, p.8; Arthur Wellesleyto Castlereagh, 31st May 1809, PRO WO 1/238.
[23] S. A. C. Cassels (ed), *Peninsula Portrait 1811 - 1814: The Letters of Captain William Bragge 3rd (Kings Own) Dragoons* (London, OUP, 1963), p.13; G. Larpent (ed), *The Private Journal of F S Larpent*, Vol. 1, p.195.
[24] L C Gurwood (ed), *General Orders of the Duke of Wellington in the Campaigns of 1809-14* (London, Clowes and Son, 1837), p.14; NAM 6807/71, p.53.
[25] W. Tomkinson, *The Diary of a Cavalry Officer 1809 - 1815* (Staplehurst, Spellmont, 1999), p.35.

CHAPTER 3
Third in Line

The British armed forces had an important role in the British economy. Globally the army and navy protected national interests and furthered colonial ambitions. In coastal areas the armed forces had become the largest purchaser of food, clothing and metal ware, while the expansion of dockyards and barracks provided employment. As a consequence an increasingly broad section of the population became interested in military affairs.

It became fashionable to read about the exploits of Britain's soldiers and sailors, their successes celebrated by days of public thanks and church bells rung to mark important victories. In 1811 Britain's expenditure on war amounted to sixteen percent of gross national product, approximately the same as that expended in 1915 at the dawn of 'total war'. It would appear that the scene was set for the army to be supported to an unprecedented level. It was not to be.

The reality for the army was that the British economic model concentrated its human resources in key industrial sectors. Agriculture and mining were favored and the extra resources produced diverted away from the armed forces and reinvested elsewhere. Economics and social stability were persistently given priority over military effectiveness. The potential benefits that the industrial and economic might of Britain could give the army could at best be only barely grasped. More often they remained tantalizingly beyond reach.

Access to capital was vital to maintaining the army. At home and overseas it was politically unacceptable for there to be a policy of the army living off the land. That elements of the army had to at times of desperation was bad enough and the results would have been politically and economically devastating if this had been consistently and deliberately applied. Capital was therefore vital in maintaining the army through the procurement of what the force required.

All of the various departments involved in maintaining the army would be involved at various stages of procurement. This could be through purchasing goods or issuing a specification for requirements. In addition to the Commissariat, four departments in particular stand out and were involved with specific items. These were the Quarter Master General (one concern of which was the supply of camping equipment), the Barrack Master General (who oversaw barracks), the Clothing board (which set the standards for uniform and oversaw its supply) and Ordnance Board (munitions production). Of the aforementioned organizations, only the Ordnance Board possessed its own production facilities, and in most cases procurement was conducted through civilian contractors.

The utilization of contractors intermeshed military organizations with private companies, making the army an important element in the British economy. For the army, contracts prevented the need to maintain production facilities. The terms of individual contracts could vary, but generally contractors would produce goods, which were then transported to army depots by either themselves or a different contractor. Distribution to the troops would then be conducted through the appropriate army organization. Local laws could have an impact on how contracts could work. This was particularly so in Portugal where a royal warrant was required to sell soap, tobacco and snuff. So as not to contravene these regulations the army itself was unable to supply these items to its troops and fourteen suppliers were contracted to supply the divisions of the British army in Portugal. As supplying these items without a contract was effectively a breach of Portuguese law, the Provost Marshal was given responsibility for enforcing and monitoring the relevant contracts.[26]

Contracts were monitored and would be lost if the contractor was found to be in breach of the terms but these terms could be particularly generous to the contractor. Those supplying forage could be able to use army stocks as an extension of their own stores. Clauses in the contract for supplying the garrison in Norwich in 1797 allowed the contractor to over deliver and then buy back or even borrow excess 'under stipulation of his returning it into store when called on for that purpose'. Under such terms the barracks become an unofficial extension to the suppliers own warehouse. The individual contracted to supply the army could therefore be seen happily removing forage from army stores to sell elsewhere.[27]

Such were the terms of contracts that the judgement if not the integrity of those awarding them come into doubt. In 1809 a contract for supplying camping equipment was awarded to a John Trotter whose uncle had been awarded the same contact in 1775. Profits were based on 10% of costs so as costs increased so too did the profit. There was little incentive for efficiency on the part of the manufacturer in such cases. That costs and the suppliers cut could fluctuate drastically prevented the fixing of prices for the army. Despite some vague answers to a Parliamentary enquiry Trotter kept the contract.[28]

Dealing with the military frequently allowed contractors to operate under special rules. This could include being exempt from certain regulations. In 1805, for example, it was ruled that the Russian, Danish and Swedish (i.e. neutral) vessels chartered by Turnball, Forbes & Co. to deliver wine to the garrison in Gibraltar could not be seized by the Royal Navy. Similarly exports of arms to Africa were exempt from certain customs inspections to avoid 'an unnecessary delay in carrying on this trade'.[29]

The manufacture and supply of munitions was primarily the responsibility of the Ordnance Board rather than civilian contractors. The organization controlled several locations concerned with the production of armaments, the most important being the Woolwich Arsenal in London. This site included a sizeable garrison to provide both defense and a workforce alongside non-military personnel. Despite such facilities the army enjoyed only limited success in meeting demand for munitions. During the summer of 1810 the Duke of Wellington was compelled to request ordnance form Portuguese stores, including 2,000 barrels of powder, 1,000 rounds of canister and 1,000 rounds of howitzer ammunition, to rectify deficiencies of British arms.[30]

It is apparent that the success of the British army in the campaigns on the European continent may have masked deficiencies in other theatres. Even units deployed in the defense of Britain and Ireland suffered from shortages of munitions, and auxiliary units raised specifically for home defense could be particularly deficient. The armament returns for three regiments stationed in Britain during 1808 are shown below.

Unit	Location	Weapon	Number Required	Shortfall
4th Drag.	Canterbury	Carbine	844	56
20th Lt. Drag	Chichester	Carbine	513	146
51st Foot	Not shown	Musket	624	57

Figure 6: Weapon deficiencies amongst three units in Britain, 1808.[31]

Unlike returns of available stores of food submitted by the Commissariat, inspection reports made by the department of the Adjutant-General highlight deficiencies as well as what was available. This allowed the army to estimate what items were required to bring units to strength, a crucial element that was lacking in Commissariat record keeping. It is apparent that deficiencies are based on the actual strength of the units concerned, not their authorized or paper strength. The result is an accurate over view of the availability of weapons to these units.

Significant numbers in all three units did not possess the required firearms. Shockingly over one quarter of the personnel of the 20th Dragoons did not possess a carbine. This is clear evidence that the army was unable to supply with the small arms they required, whether through its own output or contractors. Although these units were not in the frontline there was a realistic possibility of them becoming involved in action. There was continuous unrest across Britain during the Revolutionary and Napoleonic Wars, including food riots enclosure protests and industrial unrest. 1812 was a particularly turbulent year. Large numbers of troops were deployed to suppress disorder in northern England, more troops in fact than were sent to Portugal in 1808, while Prime Minister Spencer Perceival was assassinated in the lobby of the House of Commons. The unrest continued into the post-war period and included the Spa Fields rally (1816), the March of the Blanketeers (1817) and the Cato Street Conspiracy (1820).

There is little reason to doubt that if the economic conditions that forced the Luddites onto the streets in 1811 had taken hold a few years earlier, perhaps due to a premature outbreak of war with the United States of America or successful French occupation of Portugal, similar unrest could have occurred in 1808 and the army called on to suppress disorder. As it was the army did on occasion become involved in suppressing disorder in 1808, but only on a small scale.

Maintaining order was the most likely operation in which those forces in Britain would participate. By 1808 Britain's seemingly insurmountable naval supremacy and Napoleon's own strategic aims had focused French attention almost exclusively on the continent. Yet that the threat remained was demonstrated by the continued existence of coastal defenses. Since 1798 when French forces had reached Ireland, French naval power had been substantially reduced but it still remained capable of conducting operations. Of note is that the French fleet had been blockaded in 1798, just as it was in 1811 and 1812 when the Toulon fleet sortied. In short, it was not beyond possibility that the French could have made a landing of some form on the British coast. Anywhere from Ireland to Norfolk was a viable target. It was, however, the South East of England with its proximity to both London and French ports, that was particularly vulnerable to a 'dash' across the Channel aimed at causing maximum disruption.

There clearly existed the potential for units on home defense to become embroiled in action so the effectiveness of such units must be considered. Regarding civil disorder it appears that cavalry armed merely with sabers would be sufficient, as demonstrated bloodily at Peterloo in the post war period. An insurrection or landing would, however, have been a different matter and the experiences of the army in suppressing the Irish rebellion demonstrates that enthusiastic rebels could inflict a reverse on an ill-prepared force of regulars. Despite the relative security of Britain, therefore, it is apparent that a deficiency of munitions could have had potentially serious consequences for units deployed on home defense duties. Added to this should also be the fact that insufficiently armed units could not be sent to fight on the continent and thus had only limited utility until deficiencies could be rectified. Depriving units on home defense was thus a way of maximizing the potential of the field army but was nonetheless a dangerous gambit.

Shortages of weapons could be serious enough but the effective strength of units may have been even lower when other factors are considered. In 1808 a return of the weapons present in the 4th battalion, Royal Artillery in Canada reported firearms 'being rendered totally unfit for any further service, having been in use for twenty-two years'. Although not technologically obsolete they would have been subjected to considerable wear and weathering. Black powder weapons employed only basic mechanisms but were susceptible to the elements and even a heavy shower of rain could degrade effectiveness. That the 4th battalion had to wait so long for replacements may be attributed to its deployment in a colonial garrison - units deployed on the

European continent tended to receive priority. As demonstrated by the Canadian garrison in 1808, however, formations deployed to relatively quiet postings could soon find themselves in a war zone. Canada itself became a front line in the war against the United States four years later.[32]

Weaknesses in the infantry and cavalry could have been rectified through artillery but this was an arm in which the British army was notoriously weak. Yet again the forces deployed in defense of Britain suffered from deficiencies. The situation regarding coastal artillery in the county of Dorset during 1798 being shown below.

Status	Caliber					Total
	6lb	9lb	12lb	18lb	24lb	
Serviceable	2	18	-	11	12	43
Unserviceable	12	4	-	7	-	23
Not available	-	14	2	3	-	19
Total required	14	36	2	21	12	85
Availability	14%	50%	0%	53%	100%	50%

Figure 7: Artillery allocated to coastal defense in the county of Dorset, 1798.[33]

Taking into account guns that were unserviceable and deficient the county lacked half of the artillery considered as required for defense against French landings. This was a shocking situation considering that the survey was conducted five years after the start of hostilities, at the peak of the invasion threat.

There existed deficiencies in quantity and quality as many guns were of too small a caliber to be effective. 6-pound artillery pieces in particular were of questionable value and they were to be slowly replaced by 9-pound calibers in the field artillery units of the British arm. 6-pound pieces would largely being confined to the horse artillery where weight and thus speed of movement were as important as lethality. The trend towards 9-pounders in the field artillery is in part reflected by the limited availability of this caliber for coastal defense, while the large number of unserviceable 6-pounders reflects pieces of this caliber being removed from field duties and reallocated to other roles. The reason for the scarcity of 12-pounders was similar to that for 9-pounders. 12-pounder artillery was considered the highest practical caliber for field artillery. Of all the calibers, only the 18- and 24-pounders approached authorized strength. These calibers were too large for field use and classed as either siege or garrison artillery (the latter being their role in coastal defense).

The army failed to meet the demand for munitions due to a variety of reasons. One factor was the constant attrition to which weapons were subjected in the field. During 1808 the

Royal Artillery alone in Spain lost or had rendered unusable 355 swords, along with 375 items of associated equipment.[34] Such attrition, however, should have been easily absorbed by an industrializing nation such as Britain. That this was the case was demonstrated by the fact that, for the most part, the level of munitions supplied to the army remained relatively consistent throughout the Revolutionary and Napoleonic Wars. There is no evidence that soldiers serving in Flanders in the 1790s were significantly less armed than those serving in the Low Countries in 1815.

More significant than attrition in limiting the nation's ability to supply the army with munitions were the guiding principles of British foreign policy: the pre-eminence of the Royal Navy and the subsidizing of Britain's continental allies. There existed a fundamental imbalance in British artillery production that favored the Royal Navy in terms of quantity and quality that was to have a direct influence on the composition of the field army and its operational capability. During the siege actions of 1812 the army was compelled to rely on ordnance temporarily transferred from the fleet, and captured Russian pieces, to provide guns of the necessary caliber to pound enemy fortifications.

The armed forces of allied nations were more significant than the navy in drawing munitions away from the army. In the first three years of the Peninsular War British vessels alone delivered 200,000 muskets and 155 artillery pieces to

Spanish and Portuguese forces. Initially individual Royal Navy captains were given free reign as to who they supplied muskets. Often several hundred were landed at a in an attempt to raise bands of guerrillas. This contribution to the Allied war effort was evidence of Britain's industrial strength, yet this was only achieved at the expense of the British army. In 1810 a consignment consisting of 20,000 stands of arms (a stand consisting of a musket and associated equipment such as ammunition pouches) was dispatched to Portugal. 16,000 of these, and other 'corresponding equipment', were subsequently sent to Cadiz for allocation to Spanish forces, with only 4,000 held in reserve for British, or other allied forces, at the Tagus. Within months the British army had a shortfall of arms the Duke of Wellington would request the transfer of munitions from Portuguese stores to British forces.[35]

The army found itself competing with allied nations not only for munitions but also uniform. In the Napoleonic period military uniform symbolized many things: masculinity in portraits, military glory in art and national pride in propaganda. Dress and appearance very much represented the public face of the army and its condition was seen as a measure of how tough fighting had been during a specific campaign. A newspaper reported in February 1802 that 'different detachments of the 10th and 22nd Light Dragoons have… lately landed from Egypt, and their appearance testifies the hardships and fatigue they have undergone since they embarked at this port nearly 18 months ago'.[36]

There existed over 100 volumes relating to the regulation and administration of uniform. Being improperly dressed on parade was a court-martial offence. The provision of uniform was overseen by various bodies. These included the Clothing Board, commissions of military enquiry and various 'Boards of General Officers'. The latter were created to consider matters such as modifications to clothing and regulations. These boards were primarily drawn from a single body, which consisted of seven generals, ten lieutenant generals and two major generals. Following the Napoleonic Wars the various boards would be merged into a single body known as 'the Consolidated Board of General Officers'. Its role was described as 'the inspection and sealing of pattern articles of clothing and appointments for the army', a task for which it inherited a total of 108 books including pattern books for looping, accounts, memoranda and regulations created in 1751![37]

Despite regulations the dress of soldiers in the field was frequently far removed from that laid down in regulations. On campaign rules were often unofficially relaxed at the whim of individual officers. Of the Duke of Wellington, an individual known for conservatism, it was noted that:

[he] was a most indulgent commander... provided we brought our men into the field, well appointed, and with sixty rounds of good ammunition each, he never looked to see whether their trousers were black, blue or grey; and as ourselves, we might be rigged out in all the colours of the rainbow if we fancied it.[38]

In the 79th Foot the coats of its officers were noted as being 'black or blue of various forms', not the regulation red. During the Egyptian campaign of 1802 Egypt top hats became popular with officers due to the greater protection they offered against the sun. That such dress was the norm was demonstrated in Major General Cartwright's report on the uniform of the 4th Queen's Own Dragoons. He concluded that the standard of uniform in the regiment was good even though many of the pairs of breeches worn were not regulation issue. Besides being more colourful than allowed in Kings Regulations uniform was frequently torn, patched or outright ragged. One private wrote of his unit of his unit: 'it was difficult to tell to what regiment we belonged, for each man's coat was like Joseph's "a coat of many colours"'.[39]

Uniforms were subjected to constant attrition caused by weathering and sometimes poor quality. Footwear was particularly vulnerable to this. Of that issued to cavalry it was noted the contractor 'instead of jacking them by boiling them and beating them in the proper methods, barely stiffens them by means of some gummy substance'. Similarly of infantry boots it was noted 'the shoes finished by the contractors were so bad that in twenty four hours they were useless, the soles were very little thicker than the uppers and had paper between the soles to make them stronger. Most of the men carried their shoes in their hands'.[40]

Supplies of good quality footwear were important both aesthetically and for speed during marches, although these were not the only issues. The Duke of Wellington took a moral standpoint. It was his view that 'as the soldiers pay for the shoes they receive, it is but fair towards them that they should be of the best quality for their purpose and should fit them'.[41] Good quality boots were required to improve effectiveness and safety. This was particularly true of the cavalry arm, which, while not requiring boots designed for long marches, had other requirements. Thus in 1812 the Duke of Northumberland felt compelled to complain about the standard of boots supplied to the cavalry. In particular he highlighted that:

Jack boots properly made are the most advantageous to troopers under service, they not only save the man's legs and knees from that most severe pressure, occasioned by such horses in a charge, which I have known attended by various injurious consequences but in case of the horse falling upon his side, they are certain to save the trooper's leg being broken.[42]

Surprisingly when defective or poor quality items were

returned to the depot they were not destroyed but merely re-issued, often without modification. In 1807 a consignment of greatcoats intended to be issued to the Royal Artillery in Malta were returned as defective but were then re-issued to new recruits in Britain. A subsequent investigation reported 'it would have been better if they had been destroyed at Malta, as 'they are so bad, that battalions will not be able to profit by any of them'.[43]

With relaxed regulations on campaign uniform may have been a low priority for some soldiers. Many discarded items to lightening their packs and while in siege lines throwing shakos into the air to draw fire was a popular past time. Regulations that in theory discouraged such action included disciplinary action and charges for replacement clothing. Soldiers in the Peninsula paid 6d for a pair of boots and 6d 7s for a shirt. In many cases uniform deficiencies were caused not by destruction of the item (be it through wear, weathering or misuse) but rather the fact that items were not available. A report on the 83rd Foot described the regiment's great coats as 'entirely worn out'. This was attributed not to misuse but the poor provision of replacement clothing. Even the 4th Dragoons (850 all ranks), a unit noted as being well attired, was deficient of 154 pairs of breeches, 46 pairs of gloves, 46 hats, 3 cloaks and 32 saddles and bridles.[44]

Despite extensive regulations regarding uniform it could

be modified at the whim of officers, a practice that primarily occurred in the auxiliary forces. In September 1810 a Major B. Woodward of the Cavan Militia requested 150 bayonet belts to be supplied to the unit. This purchase was to be made at Woodward's own expense of 5d per belt 'for the purpose of fastening by the accoutrements in the quick movements of the light infantry'. The request was refused because according to Commissary General Handfield 'only an order from the Lord Lieutenant [can allow] any article of store to be disposed of'. Handfield advised Woodward that he could purchase the items he requested at the next sale of surplus equipment. It was stock control, not uniform regulation, that hindered this modification to clothing. A unit of the British army could not obtain equipment from stores, but through the auction of surplus equipment such items were available to civilians in Ireland, a country in which armed insurrection was perceived as a near constant threat! That Woodward sought to improve the effectiveness of his command is also commendable. It would, however, have taken considerable training as well as the correct equipment for a light infantry role.[45]

Regulations stipulated considerable variation between uniforms of different formations. This was particularly so of tunics and the diversity did little to improve their supply. A company's designation as line, light or grenadier dictated the arrangement of its lace and shoulder decoration. Tunic colours were broadly divided into red for the infantry, blue or red for cavalry and blue for the supporting arms, although there were variations (most famously the green of the Rifle Brigade) and the facing colour of regiments also varied (this being the colouring of the cuffs and collar). Details concerning colours could be confused and the commanding officer of the 4th Dragoons was unsure whether his holsters should have been black or bearskin.[46]

In the case of munitions the army was involved in procurement through issuing specifications (the war office) and manufacture (arsenals), while the production of uniforms was merely directed by the army. The situation regarding accommodation and shelter was that the organizations concerned not only issued specifications (be they for the construction of structures or supply of associated items) but were also actively involved in both maintenance and administration. It was the task of the Adjutant-General's department and commanding officers, rather than the clothing boards, to compile returns of uniform, while barrack masters themselves reported on the condition of barracks maintained by the Barrack Master General's department.

Accommodation and shelter in the army during the period can be divided in to the categories of permanent (barracks), temporary (tents and shelter provided by the army) and field (any shelter considered expedient).

Responsibility for providing the latter frequently rested with the over worked commissaries. Such individuals were expected to be familiar with all the resources required by the army in their area. Troops, however, also relied on their own ingenuity for such shelter, creating shelters from blankets, branches and anything else available. The result was that whole villages could be stripped to provide building materials for makeshift shelters and fuel. The practice was to become so widespread that in 1811 general orders were issued in an attempt to limit such activity. Away from the frontline, when troops tended to be less mobile, the allocation of shelter and associated items, such as fuel, could be better controlled. Indeed, soldiers of all ranks could find themselves billeted in the home of a local civilian.

In Spain and Portugal the practice of billeting with civilians was popular amongst many locals as those most commonly accommodated in this way were officers, the presence of whom were believed to deter looting. The validity of such a belief was seemingly demonstrated during the storming of Badajoz. Lieutenant Grattan of the Connaught Rangers was invited to dine in a house at this time and he wrote, 'all outside was noise and pillage [but] affairs within went on agreeably enough'. While Grattan wined and dined the British army outside embarked on an orgy of looting. The arrival of officers in homes was not always welcome and they could prove to be less than gracious guests. A Captain Browne, for example, instructed his servant to steal clothing from his Spanish host. For the rank and file local accommodation tended to be a crowded barn or peasant dwelling. This could be an unpleasant experience for all and at least one Commissary deliberately billeted troops in the properties of locals he disliked.[47]

The billeting of troops in local properties was not unique to overseas deployments. During the early stages of the Revolutionary Wars it had been common practice in Britain to billet troops at local inns and even in local homes. As in Spain such billeting was not always popular. This was particularly so in 1809, when large numbers of officers suffering from fever contracted in Walcheren were understandably but cold heartedly refused accommodation by the citizens of Harwich.[48]

The blow to innkeepers in Britain was partly softened by the payment of generous financial compensation. This amounted to 12d to 16d per cavalryman with horse, 6d if without a horse, 10s 6d per chaplain and his horse and 4d per infantryman. In addition to these payments, innkeepers also received money described as being 'in lieu of beer' directly from the War Office. It was of course one thing for soldiers to participate in an occasional fracas while drunk, but the billeting of troops in inns also significantly increased the danger of them becoming involved in more serious politically motivated, even revolutionary, disorder. Partly in response to this threat and also in response to the expanding army, the government of Prime Minister William Pitt instigated a barrack building programme.

Barracks were the responsibility of the Barrack Department. Barrack masters oversaw individual barracks and their role was to ensure the blocks were properly equipped and maintained. Like the Commissariat they operated in accordance with a system of regular returns, including monthly, four-monthly and six-monthly reports. In barracks the rooms of officers were equipped almost solely as a place to sleep. The inventory of an officers room would have contained few items beyond bedding, fuel for a fire and a wash bowl. Some may have enjoyed the addition of a desk and chair. Captains were allocated individual rooms, while two subalterns or staff officers shared a single room. Figure 8 compares the rooms of officers and the other ranks in 1797. It can be seen that one of the primary differences between the two was the provision of cooking implements, including a wide variety of pots and pans for the ORs. Conspicuous by its absence from the list of officers' furniture is bedding, although other sources indicate its presence. The rooms of the other ranks were clearly intended for use by far greater numbers of men, and the rooms also contained lower-quality bedding materials – primarily straw and sacking. A notable and perhaps concerning omission from the rooms of other ranks is chamber pots and similar!

Rooms of officers	Rooms of other ranks	
Tables	Fire irons	Wooden ladles
Chairs	Fenders	Large bowls
Fire irons	Iron pots	Large platters
Fenders	Iron boilers	Small bowls
Coal scuttles	Pot covers	Trenchers
Bellows	Boiler covers	Spoons
Coal trays	Iron works	Tin beer cans
Mops	Coppers	Tin drinking cups
Hair Brooms	Pot hooks	Candle sticks
Earthen salting pans	Hand hooks	Water buckets
Urine tubs	Trivets	Blankets
Chamber pots	Flesh forks	Sacking
Coal baskets	Frying pans	Cordial
	Grid Irons	Round towels
	Iron ladles	

Figure 8: An inventory of furniture and utensils in a barracks, c1797.[49]

While barracks helped house the army at home and in major garrisons, accommodation for troops in the field varied between woefully inadequate and non-existence. The solution was to expand the provision of camping equipment. The department with primary responsibility for this was the Quarter Master General.

The first and on occasion only line of defense for a

soldier against the elements was his blanket. This was assuming that it had not already been traded for alcohol, warmer clothes or discarded to save weight. The blanket could be used either conventionally or as part of a crude shelter, supported by muskets. The latter role was facilitated by the introduction of a reinforced ring in the corner of army blankets. Not all soldiers enjoyed even this basic protection from the elements. Until 1810 only half to three quarters of infantry serving in the Peninsula had been issued with these special blankets. In addition the erection of the makeshift shelter was unpopular because it provided little protection during cold nights. A more substantial solution than the blanket shelter was the round tent, which was initially developed for use in Flanders but officially issued to all British forces from 1811. In practice many units received them much later than this or not at all, and there were often sufficient tents available only if absentees, servants and sentries were discounted. The Peninsula army was so used to sleeping rough that upon their return in 1814 many veterans were unable to sleep in even a crude bed.

Be it for tents, guns or uniform, it is clear that Britain's economic and industrial capability was not fully exploited to support the army. This was not the result of a concerted policy to keep the army in check through deliberately failing to meet its needs. Rather it was a question of priority. The first hurdle confronting the army was the attitude of both the state and society towards the military and war, conflict being seen as disruptive to the economy. The proportion of output allocated to fighting the Napoleonic Wars, however, demonstrates a willingness on the part of the Britain to meet the challenge of war. The difficulty facing the army was thus not one of resources committed to the war in general, but the proportion of these resources that it would receive. Regarding this the force faced not only competition with the Royal Navy but also the armies of other countries. Therefore, the army did not necessarily receive a fair share of the resources allocated to the national war effort. Those that it did receive often could not be exploited due to policy. The need to comply with regulations was not necessarily compatible with operational necessity and the benefits of using contractors was diluted by corruption and incompetence.

---

[26] Extracts from General Orders, Cartaxo 28th February 1811, NAM 6807/221, pp.5-7.
[27] Singer to Heathy, Commissary General's office, 25th March 1806; Malisses to G. Bimiy, Commissary General's Office, 9th June 1810, PRO WO 63/45.
[28] *Eighth Report of Military Enquiry* (London, Office of the Secretary at War, 1809), pp.227-8.
[29] Draft of Instructions to the High Court of Admiralty Respecting Vessels

Belonging to Russia, Denmark or Sweden, 2nd February, 1805; Privy Council Miscellaneous Unbound Papers; Privy Council to (Illegible), 17th August 1813, PRO PC 1/3643, /4013.

[30] Council Chamber, Whitehall, 2nd March 1816, PRO PC 1/4087; J MacLeod to Mulgrave, Woolwhich, 17th February 1812, PRO WO 55/1369, Adjutant General's Confidential Letters (Outward), September 1810 to February 1816;; Wellington to Liverpool, Alvera, 22nd August 1810, PRO WO 1/245.

[31] PRO WO 27/92/1, Office of Commander in Chief and War Office: Adjutant General and Army Council Inspections, 1808.

[32] Major-General Stead to Crew, Woolwich, 9th May 1808, PRO WO 55/1314, Letters to Board of Ordnance from Adjutant General, February 1807 to July 1809.

[33] PRO WO 30/116, Report on the Coast of Dorsetshire, 1798, p.17.

[34] Macleod to Crew, Woolwich, 22nd May 1809, PRO WO 55/1314.

[35] Wellington to Liverpool, Cartaxo, 12th January 1811, PRO WO 1/248; Wellington to Liverpool, Alvera, 22nd August 1810,PRO WO 1/245.

[36] *Salisbury Journal*, 15th February 1802, p.2.

[37] Minutes of the Proceedings of the Board of General Officers, 13th March 1811, PRO WO 377/2, Various Papers, 1809 upon the System of Clothing and Off Reckonings for the Army; Draft Warrant, 1816, PRO WO 43/296, Amalgamation of Boards of General Officers with Inspectorate of Clothing to form the Consolidated Board

[38] W. Grattan, *Adventures with the Connaught Rangers, 1809 - 1814* (London, Greenhill, 1989), p.50.

[39] NAM 6807/71, Notebook of Lieutenant John Ford 1808 – 12, p.133; Major General Cartwright's confidential report on the actual state of the 4th Queen's Own Dragoons, 7th May 1808, PRO WO 27/92/1; B. H. Liddell – Hart (ed), *The Letters of Private Wheeler 1809 - 1828* (London, Michael Joseph, 1951), p.74.

[40] Duke of Northumberland to Lieutenant Colonel Hill, Alnwick Castle 4th February 1812, NAM 6309/138, Various Letters from the Duke of Northumberland; Memoirs of Captain Peter Jennings, NAM 8301/102, no page number or other reference and the passage is included on a separate, undated, sheet.

[41] Wellington to Liverpool, 31st March, 1811, PRO WO 1/248.

[42] Duke of Northumberland to Lieutenant Colonel Hill, Alnwick Castle 4th February 1812, NAM 6309/138.

[43] Macleod to Crew, Woolwich, 5th March 1807, PRO WO 55/1314.

[44] Standing Orders, Order No 27, NAM 6807/221, p.5; Half Yearly Report of 83rd Regiment, Cape of Good Hope, NAM 6112/78, Wetherall Papers, Inspection Returns and Correspondence of Major General F. A. Wetherall, p.15; Returns of clothing and accoutrements of the 4th Queen's Own Dragoons, 7th May 1808, PRO WO 27/92/1.

[45] Major B. Woodward to Major Ramsey, Royal Barracks, 17th September 1810; Commissary General Charles Handfield to Major B. Woodward, Commissary

General's Office, 19th September 1810, PRO WO 63/91.

[46] Major General Cartwright's confidential report on the actual state of the 4th Queen's Own Dragoons, 7th May 1808, PRO WO 27/92/1.

[47] Grattan, *Adventures with the Connaught Rangers*, p161; R. N. Buckley (ed), *The Napoleonic War Journal of Captain Thomas Henry Browne 1807 - 1816* (London, Army Records Society, 1987), p.181; A. L. F. Schauman, *On the Road with Wellington* (London, William Heinemann, 1924), p.76.

[48] Dent to Mother, Colchester, 12th September 1809, NAM 7008/11/2. The fact that they had to seek accommodation of this nature is further evidence of the limitations of the barrack building program.

[49] *Letter from Barrak* [sic] *Master General to Barrak Masters* (Barraks Office, 1797), Appendix.

CHAPTER 4
From A to B: Transport

Food, tents, guns and uniforms. All of them relied on wagons to get from manufacturers to depots and from depots to the front line. Britain boasted an unrivalled transport network of roads and canals. Naval supremacy stretched this reach further but this infrastructure would inevitably be hampered by geography. It was the state of the roads in continental warzones, not turnpikes in Britain, that would determine the effectiveness of transport operations. Unlike its continental counterparts it was also hoped that the army would never enjoy the benefits of home soil.

For all the advantages of Britain's infrastructure there existed rules preventing its effective utilisation. Troops arriving in an area were required to present a warrant to be signed by a magistrate. In theory this ensured that bodies of soldiers troops remained under civilian supervision while moving through an area. Quite what a magistrate could have done to stop a battalion intent on anarchy is not clear. The army benefited as troops would not become lost (possibly ending up at the nearest inn). The weakness of the system was that it could only operate if the correct papers were presented. If this did not occur magistrates were able to refuse a force passage. This was the case in June 1807 when a column of wagons carrying supplies for the artillery arrived unexpectedly at the Sussex town of Winchelsea. As he had not been informed of their pending arrival the local magistrate refused them passage and sent the column on a detour around the town, resulting in a four hour delay.[50]

Until 1795 the army had little integral transport capability of note and relied on civilian contractors. These contracts were not administered by central government but local magistrates. In October 1803 it was agreed that contractors in Wiltshire would receive 1s per mile for wagons, with an additional 3d if towed by four horses or six oxen, while payments for carts were to be 9d per mile, with an additional 2d for four horses or oxen.[51]

In 1795 the Corps of Royal Waggoners was created to support the transport needs of the army. Like most of the other forces deployed by Britain to Flanders performance was less than adequate. The corps was soon disbanded but in 1799 the Royal Wagon Corps, latterly the Royal Wagon Train, was formed. Its pathetically small size ensured that it too met with little success but the army had taken its first steps towards a permanent force of military drivers. It was the view of Arthur Wellesley that this formation only became effective following the absorption of the Irish Wagon Train following the 1800 Act of Union. While this event may have improved the force civilians continued to man most of the wagons used by the army.[52]

When the British army deployed to Spain in 1808 little thought was given to transportation. There was a belief that the vehicles and personnel of the Royal Wagon Train, in conjunction with allied armies, would be sufficient to meet the logistical needs of the army. This belief proved to be extremely optimistic and steps were taken to improve the situation through the utilization of local oxen. It was fitting that a significant number of these locally procured oxen found themselves drawing local carts. These carts did not benefit from the advances made in transport technology in Britain and were poorly produced using square axles. This gave them a distinctive sound which was described as a 'voice that could be heard a mile off'.[53]

The majority of those who drove the carts were Portuguese and Spanish muleteers. The initial impression of them was often less than favorable and they soon gained a reputation for laziness and desertion. No doubt influenced by cultural stereotypes the detractors of the muleteers were soon proved wrong. Praise for them came from a source unafraid to criticize or highlight failure. Arthur Wellesley wrote of the muleteers that they were exhausted after having 'made an exertion against the enemy by the assistance which they have given to me'. This was gushing praise by the standards of the man who would become Duke of Wellington.[54]

Muleteers were not second-class personnel and a

muleteer occupied the same position in the military hierarchy as an English fighting soldier of that rank. Muleteers were divided into sections under their own corporals (capatrasses) who were responsible for distributing rations. Orders issued in 1811 instructed that soldiers escorting mules to the rear were there purely as escorts, it being advised to select 'one steady man' for each column. Soldiers assigned to such duties were instructed to 'not force [the muleteers] to march faster or further than the capatraz is inclined to go'. Muleteers were quite correctly viewed as experts in caring for the animals in their charge and it was even proposed that they should retain ownership of mules to ensure the animals received the best treatment.[55]

The Wagon Train and muleteers were not the sole operators of wagons in the army. Regiments held a number for duties including the distributing supplies from regimental depots, carrying wounded and administrative tasks. Commissaries accompanying units used a wagon for the carriage of ledgers, while Paymasters often commandeered vehicles against regulations to ease the carriage of pay books. The difference between the Wagon Train and other wagon users was the capability to maintain them. Organizations such as the Quartermaster's Department and Commissariat hired civilians, on contracts of varying length, to maintain their wagons. The train employed its own specialist personnel. Personnel employed by the Royal Wagon Train on maintenance duties were recorded as artificers and included blacksmiths, cotton weavers, wheelwrights, collar makers and farriers.[56]

Other organizations lacked the specialist maintenance personnel of the Train. A highly critical report of October 1811 noted of those employed in other formations:

[they] are able to perform the smallest repair on the cart but in clumsiest manner, and are wholly ignorant how to refit it, in case of serious accident – the very repairs thus made by [them], from being so clumsily performed, prove a means of tearing to pieces and ultimately demolishing a cart… in the event of a wheel being broken, these carts remain totally unserviceable unless a wheel man can be obtained.[57]

An additional specialist appointment, although not one unique to the Royal Wagon Train, was the post of Veterinary Surgeon (who was, in theory, also assigned a deputy). The train went for three years (1803 – 1806) without a veterinary surgeon and the deputy filled the role. This occurred during a relatively quiet period for the army and does not appear to have unduly affected the operational capabilities of the organization. Finally, the skills of the drivers themselves should not be underestimated. The report of October 1811 stated that 'no wheeled carriage can be securely drawn over an [sic] hilly country for even one march, especially when drawn by horses little accustomed to draught, and under the charge of men wholly ignorant of governing horses'. It is contentious whether the personnel of the Train were better than the Spanish muleteers. The evidence is that the converse was the case. Their skills, however, were far in excess of the average soldier and the washed out cavalry men from which they were first recruited.[58]

The Royal Wagon Train was divided into troops, a reflection of its cavalry heritage. The number and composition of the troops were not constant and reflected changes in operational requirements.

Year	Number of Active Troops	Year	Number of active troops
1800	8	1809	12
1801	8	1810	11
1802	6	1811	10
1803	4	1812	10
1804	11	1813	21
1805	12	1814	19
1806	12	1815	12
1807	11	1816	12
1808	11	1817	5

Figure 9: Active Troops in the Royal Wagon Train.[59]

Upon its formation in 1799 the train was based at Canterbury and consisted of three troops. Its commander was Colonel Digby Hamilton, who would remain in command of the regiment for the duration of the war.

In 1800 manpower and capabilities were significantly increased by the absorption of the Irish Wagon Train as a result of the 1801 Act of Union. This more than doubled the number of active troops and introduced experienced personnel. The effect of this was relatively short lived due to the so called Peace of Amiens in 1802. This was little more than a lull in the conflict between Britain and France. Historians use it as convenient point to mark the end of the Revolutionary Wars and the beginning of the Napoleonic. For a short sighted and budget conscious army it was an excuse to make savings. The force was reduced to a meagre number of four active troops. Strength soon recovered but capability lagged behind.

The Wagon Train was to remain based at Canterbury until 1803, when its headquarters were moved to Croydon Barracks. The year 1804 would see a significant improvement in the structure of the train, the creation of so called depot troops. Using fewer and simpler wagons, these were smaller, self-contained troops used to support units and garrisons, rather than the system of ad hoc detachments that had characterized the earlier deployments. The flexibility of the Train was further improved by the addition of a Lieutenant Colonel. This would prove valuable when the Train would effectively be split into two – the Royal Wagon Train at Croydon and the Royal Wagon Train in the

Peninsula. This administrative division was significant and set a precedent for the future overseas deployments of the organization.

Even when split between Britain and Flanders during the campaigns of 1793 to 1799 the Train had functioned as an administrative whole. There was one headquarters (at Canterbury) that collated the returns of all the troops. This practice continued when the detachments of the Royal Wagon Train first arrived in Spain and Portugal during the course of 1808. During this time the returns of relevant units were listed as footnotes in returns of total strength. By 1809 the force had grown from a number of detachments to complete troops and returns for the Royal Wagon Train in the Iberian Peninsula were collated by a headquarters established at Lisbon.

In March 1810 five of the Train's nine were operating in Spain and Portugal. Of the troops, four were based at Leira and one at Rio Mayor, while a small detachment was deployed to Belem. The number of officers was subject to some fluctuation and many were in the theatre for varying periods of time. In September 1810 the 'Detachment of the Royal Wagon Train in Spain and Portugal', as the force became known, reached the peak at which it was to remain until 1814. Two quartermasters operated with the Train in the Peninsula while typically only one such officer had been on the strength of the Royal Wagon Train in Britain. This force provided the core of the 'Detachment Royal Wagon Train in France' that served in that country during 1814. The practice of collating returns by theatre continued, with overseas forces being referred to as 'detachments operating in'. It was a term that downplayed the significance of these deployments in the context of the train's overall operational capability. By 1815 the most important overseas detachments of the organization were located in the Peninsula, France (including the army of occupation) and Hanover.

By necessity the elements of the Royal Wagon Train based in Britain were seen as being of secondary importance to the force deployed to Europe. Their capability reflected this. The Royal Wagon Train in Britain during this period was split between depots in Hythe, Canterbury, the Isle of White and Portsmouth. None were based at headquarters in Croydon, demonstrating the split that had occurred between operations and administration. By this stage of the conflict the majority of the organization's formations operating in Britain were so called depot troops, as opposed to the better-equipped marching troops deployed to the Peninsula. Depot troops operated 18 wagons, compared to 30 in the marching troops, the later including forage wagons. Taking into consideration the number of depot troops deployed in Britain, it is apparent that the force deployed to Spain and Portugal represented the cream of the organization in terms of both quantity and quality.

In March 1810 the Train was effectively at full stretch, with its main operational elements serving in the Iberian Peninsula and only a reserve existing in Britain. If necessary the depot troops could have formed a core around which additional troops could be raised in an emergency, but not without weakening the units deployed at home. By this stage of the war the Royal Wagon Train based in Britain, while maintaining a similar number of troops, was actually weaker than during the peace of Amiens when it had been drastically reduced (a strength of approximately 200 in 1810 compared to 250 in 1802).[60]

The increase in the number of wagons operated by the Train brought with it greater demand for draught animals. Traditionally these had been horses and such was the Royal Wagon Train's reliance on this animal that its administration shared much in common with the cavalry. Returns were compiled on preprinted forms designed for cavalry regiments, with unnecessary words and references crossed out. At times the needs of the Train would even be met by transferring animals from fighting units, a practice that was particularly desirable given that the cost of purchasing horses in Britain rose continually during the period.[61]

The number of animals transferred between formations could be considerable. 150 draught animals intended for General Spencer's artillery brigade in Portugal in August 1808 were reallocated to General Burrard for logistical tasks after their late arrival. Embarrassingly the artillery would subsequently be forced to abandon guns due to lack of transport! Just as concerning was the large number of horses purchased for combat use but found unsuitable. Major General Cartwright noted that some horses employed by the 4th (Queen's Own) Dragoons were too big for cavalry duties (being more suited to pulling wagons), while in April 1809 Arthur Wellesley had wrote to Castelreagh expressing concern that even the regiments of guards had on their strength horses that were unsuitable for combat duty. It seems the army frequently fell victim to unscrupulous horse traders. Who had been involved in purchasing many of the animals in 1808 to 1809? Lieutenant Colonel Hamilton, commander of the Royal Wagon Train[62]

In defense of Hamilton and other horse purchasers desperation may have played a role. Often there was barely sufficient sea transportation for the cavalry horses, let alone the animals required by the Royal Wagon Train. The difficulties encountered when moving horses to war zones was demonstrated by the instructions given to General Sir John Moore upon his arrival in Spain during 1808:

the cavalry you will... direct to move by land and if the horses for the artillery can take the same route so as to admit the whole of the horse transports being returned to England, it will tend much to accelerate the arrival of the cavalry from home.

In short transports were badly needed elsewhere and Moore had to make do (which pretty well characterized the whole British campaign in Spain during 1808). British naval superiority had got him there but in regards to moving horses by sea Moore was on his own. [63]

Interestingly the orders given to Moore made no mention of the animals of the train. With the army established in the Peninsula after 1809, the situation regarding horse transports was still precarious. Colonel Bambury of the artillery wrote there were a number of 'horses waiting for a conveyance to Portugal' and that 'as soon as cavalry transports are at our disposal, sufficient tonnage will be allotted to the horses in question; but their embarkation has been delayed by the total want of the means of transporting them'. The Duke of Wellington also complained of transport vessels being requisitioned for other duties by the transport board. The simple fact of the matter was that with three organizations competing for space aboard horse transports (the regiments of cavalry, Royal Artillery and Royal Wagon Train) none of them would ever have adequate space allocated.[64]

Fortunately for the Train shortages of horses could in part be rectified by utilizing mules and shortages of these by oxen. Manpower, however, was a different prospect. The focus of recruitment, as for the infantry and cavalry, were the recruiting parties. These differed from those of the combat arms being containing fewer officers and promising a much smaller bounty for recruitment. In 1802 recruits to the Royal Wagon Train would receive only £6 2s, compared to £13 5s for infantrymen. Infantrymen were also eligible for an extra bounty if transferring from the militia or volunteers (amounting to £7 12s 6d). As the war progressed recruitment bounties for the train were significantly reduced, with the result that by January 1814 the Royal Wagon Train bounty payment amounted to only £4 4s, while in 1816 it fell to £3 14s.

The Royal Wagon Train was relatively easier to join than the infantry as there was a lower height requirement than for the combat fighting arms. In 1808 this was only five feet one inch for the train, compared to five feet five inches for the infantry and five feet seven inches for the cavalry. It could also be said that service in the Train was a soft option and service took a lesser toll on its personnel. At the headquarters of the Peninsular army in October 1810 276 personnel of the Royal Wagon Train were present. Of these 19 (approximately 7%) were listed as sick. The figures for infantry was 17%, the cavalry 25% and the artillery 24%. Despite such evidence, however, service in the Train was not without hardships.[65]

The role of the Royal Wagon Train dictated that it was continually active. Bad weather that forced fighting regiments to return to cantonments or remain in barracks was not allowed to hinder activities. This was demonstrated in December 1811 when a detachment form the Train in Ireland was ordered to deliver materials vital to the war effort: a general's furniture. Braving some of the worse snows on record the detachment found roads blocked and horses rapidly exhausted. All the while logistical activity by the Commissariat in that part of Ireland had been curtailed due the severe weather.[66]

The great irony of the Royal Wagon Train was that it was too small to meet the needs of the wartime army, yet, too large for peace. Its strength was drastically reduced after 1815 and had Napoleon not returned from exile it would have been reduced at least a year sooner. In January 1816 the strength of the Royal Wagon Train stood at fifteen troops. Three of which were listed as foreign (primarily consisting of Germans) and by May were amalgamated into a single troop. Within a month strength was further reduced. In April there had been 169 privates in the foreign troops, by June 1816 there were a mere 17. As the British army has so often done over the years, it dismissed those foreigners in its service as rapidly as they had volunteered.[67]

The hatchet of post-war reductions did not of course fall solely on the foreign units of the Royal Wagon Train. The whole organization was rapidly and brutally gutted; its manpower and equipment disposed of. In February 1816 there were approximately NCOs and other ranks. This fell to 840 in November and 745 in February 1817. Reductions were almost exclusively achieved by cutting the force in Britain. Overseas strength was concentrated in the Army of Occupation in France. By the end of 1817, of the Trains 761 horses 711 were in France, along 75% of the Train's artificers.[68]

By November 1816 there was only one active troop in Britain compared to four in France. This solitary troop in Britain demonstrated the significant improvements that had occurred in the Train since its formation seventeen years earlier. In terms of personnel this one troop, 166 strong, was equivalent to the three active troops that accounted for the main element of the Royal Wagon Train in the summer of 1799. It employed eleven artificers, more than the total available in 1799. The Train of 1816 also operated a variety of wagons, designated as sprung, bread and forage. That only one troop existed did not unduly influence its flexibility. Still based at Croydon Barracks, the Royal Wagon Train continued to maintain detachments at Hythe, Sandhurst and on the Isle of Wight.

---

[50] Minutes of 2nd February 1808, WSRO B18/100/7, Salisbury Division, Justices Minute Books, January 1808 to January 1809; Macleod to Crew, Woolwich, 17th June 1807, PRO WO 55/1314.
[51] *Salisbury Journal*, 31 October 1803, p.1.
[52] Arthur Wellesley to Castlereagh, 8 August 1808, PRO WO 1/228.
[53] Grenville Eliot to Wife, Llavos, 7th August 1808, NAM 5903/127/6, letters of William Grenville Eliot, R.A.
[54] Villa Formosa, 10th December 1811, Extracts from General Orders, NAM 6807/221, pp.12-13.
[55] Standing Orders, Order No. 37, NAM 6807/221, p.8; Villa Formosa, 10th December 1811, Extracts from General Orders, NAM 6807/221, pp.12-13; PRO WO 37/10/26, paragraph 17.
[56]. PRO WO 12/1522, Royal Wagon Train 1799 – 1801.
[57] PRO WO 37/10/26, paragraphs 5 to 6.
[58] PRO WO 17/54/1, Monthly returns of the Royal Wagon Train; PRO WO 37/10/26, paragraph 9.
[59] Royal Wagon Train monthly pay lists, PRO WO 12/1522 to WO 12/1526.
[60] Return of officers, non-commissioned officers, men and horses detached from headquarters of the Royal Wagon Train, Croydon, March 1810, PRO WO 17/54/1.
[61] Certificate of Commanding Officer Lieutenant Colonel Digby Hamilton, April 1802, PRO WO 12/1523.
[62] A. Wellesley to Sir Harry Burrard, Aeyria, 11 August 1808, PRO WO 1/228; Return of horses received by the Royal Wagon Train, March 1810, PRO WO 17/54/2; Major General Cartwright's confidential report on the actual state of the 4th Queen's Own Dragoons, 7 May 1808, PRO WO 27/92/1; Wellesley to Castlereagh, Lisbon, 29 April 1809, PRO WO 1/238.
[63] To Moore, Downing Street, 26 September 1808, PRO WO 1/236.
[64] Colonel Bambury to MacLeod, Downing Street, 6 February 1810, PRO WO55/1369; Wellington to Liverpool, Celario, 18 August 1810, PRO WO 1/245.
[65] Bounty payments, 1802, PRO WO 17/2813, Monthly returns of the British army at home and abroad, Jan 1803 - Aug 1805, with at front, scale of age and standards for recruits, 1802-1808, and scale of bounty, 1802-1823; Royal Wagon Train monthly pay list, January 1814 to January 1816, PRO WO 12/1529 and WO 12/1530; General return, WO1/246, War Department in Letters and Papers 1810, f.1.
[66] Brackets in original. N. Malasses to Robert Colvill [sic], Commissary General's Office, 4th February 1811, PRO WO 63/45.
[67] Royal Wagon Train monthly pay list, April 1816, PRO WO 12/12017, Royal Wagon Train Foreign Corps, 1816.
[68] Royal Wagon Train monthly pay list, February 1816 to November 1817, PRO

WO 12/1530.

CHAPTER 5

A moral dimension

Warfare is a strange business. Modern nations have come to realize that it is one thing to expend their soldiers' lives on the battlefield, quite another not to look after them beforehand. Whether this is through genuine morality or guilt is open to debate. In either case, the idea is not as recent as may be inferred from the bloody nature of eighteenth and nineteenth century warfare. Generals may have been more reckless with the lives of their soldiers' in the wars against France but even before this they had become well aware of the need to nurture these troops. Military personnel represented an investment that had to be nurtured, with states taking a growing interest in their welfare. Put simply a happy workforce is an effective workforce.

One of the great challenges faced by the army was not the welfare of soldiers themselves so much as the welfare of soldiers' dependents. For reasons that are not entirely clear the army believed that men with families would make better soldiers. The Duke of Wellington certainly believed that not recruiting them encouraged 'the worst description of men to enter the service'. A potentially important reason for men with families not to enlist was economics. Enlistment could take away the main provider of a family's income and it was not always easy for families to remain together - at the outbreak of the Revolutionary and Napoleonic Wars the army made little provision for families to travel with soldiers. The regulations concerning this referred only to wives as it was assumed any children would also accompany them.[69]

It was relatively easy for wives to follow husbands serving in Britain and, despite the fact that married quarters and similar provision for wives did not exist until the mid-nineteenth century, families could remain together or at least in proximity due to the practice of billeting troops at inns (a practice that became less common as more barracks were constructed). When travelling overseas the army allowed a restricted number of wives and their children to follow each regiment. In such circumstances the army allowed for only six wives to travel with each infantry company or cavalry troop, while in the Royal Artillery the allocation was a more generous eight and ten for foot and horse batteries respectively. Rations were established as being half that of a man's for women and one third for children.[70]

Only the wives of privates and non-commissioned officers were permitted to travel with the regiments to foreign postings at the expense of the army, while commissioned officers frequently paid for their wives to travel with them. Others married local women while on service, despite the fact that since 1685 permission had been required from a soldier's commanding officer for him to marry. The result was that a large number of women and children followed regiments while they were deployed overseas. With the 25th Light Dragoon Regiment in India during the latter stages of the war there were no less than seventy-two women, thirty-one of whom were non-European.[71]

Whether widowed or married there was initially little provision made for the women who followed the army as it travelled between overseas postings. Left to fend for themselves they inevitably turned to looting. In August 1812 the Duke of Wellington remarked that 'the followers of the army, the Portuguese women in particular, must be prevented by the provosts from plundering the gardens and fields of vegetables'. Thus the army found itself on the horns of a dilemma in regard to women and children. They were seen to hamper the supply of the army by consuming food and taking up transport; conversely the army wanted men with families and wives performed useful duties such as nursing and foraging.[72]

The army acknowledge that whatever their overall impact, wives would always follow the army and legislation was required to accommodate this fact of life. In 1811 an act 'for enabling the wives and families of soldiers embarked on foreign service' was introduced. This effectively provided an allowance for families to return home, being extended to include widows in 1812 and regiments embarking in Ireland in 1818. Following the end of the Peninsular Campaign in 1814 it was the army's policy to encourage Spanish and Portuguese women to return to their own homes rather than follow their husbands back to Britain but this was not strictly enforced. In 1814 a limited number of foreign wives, selected with 'the greatest caution' were allowed back to Britain. Thus, during 1816 some 44 women and 27 children, who had been following the 88th Regiment on the continent, were allowed to return with their husbands.

First proposed in 1811, wives, widows, children and orphans were eventually allowed to draw food from army stockpiles in 1818. Until 1846 many of these regulations continued to be applied even if the child was born out of wedlock, a relatively enlightened policy for the era. Although rudimentary, the army operated a system of welfare for the families of its soldiers.[73]

The army was an organization noted for its conservatism but in its policies towards families was moving much more rapidly than the state towards a welfare system. This was also evident in regard to education. The availability of education was one of the most tangible advantages offered by a career in the army and children would benefit as an off shoot of programs intended to educate the rank and file. The subject of educating soldiers was a source of some debate; one contemporary arguing that service in the army alone was sufficient, due to 'the beneficial influence of moderate instruction and impressing the mind with a due sense of moral and religious duty'.[74] Such a view was not common and formal education in the British army had a history stretching as far back as 1675, when the first army school was created in the Tangiers garrison.

The growth in the number of army schools was not rapid but the barrack building program enabled permanent schools to be established in most regiments by 1809. The purpose of these schools was to educate soldiers but it was common for their children to be taught in them when the regiment was away. Initially the provision of such education was at the whim of regimental colonels although a standard structure was soon adopted and it was noted that the school of the 80th Regiment in particular paid great attention to the children of the regiment.[75]

The Duke of York was a keen advocate of education in the army, for both soldiers and their children alike, and he considered the cost of schools to be 'trifling compared to the benefits [of] attending such an establishment'. Both a royal son and a bumbling general, York's tenure as commander in chief could have easily been one of stagnation yet he oversaw notable advances in the field of army education. Particularly important was the formalization of regimental school administration in 1811. The reform required each battalion to appoint a sergeant-school-master, paid at the rate of a paymaster's clerk. Schools were also to be allocated a room in each barracks and funded from regimental budgets. Significantly this was to be available to soldiers and children.

Besides York's reforms, the Royal Military Asylum at Chelsea and its sister institution at Dover were both clear indications of the army's commitment to a policy that emphasized education, at a time when it is estimated that only 15% of the population received any schooling. The establishment at Chelsea was funded by the state and in 1812 received a grant of £20,000. Conversely civilian schools tended to be funded by charities and philanthropists, not receiving significant state funding until 1831 in Ireland and 1833 in Britain.[76]

While a soldier's family could benefit while he served, there was the difficulty of what would happen once service ended. Pensions for soldiers had existed for centuries as a means to prevent soldiers from becoming involved in unrest. There is perhaps nothing more unnerving for a government than an uprising led by well trained, potentially well-armed, and annoyed subjects. By the time of the Napoleonic Wars there was a growing realization that expansion of the army increased the likelihood of this. Pensions were a means of keeping old soldiers content.

Besides placating former soldiers there was also

recognition that pensions could serve as a means to increase the appeal of the army as a career. Yet again the army lagged behind the Royal Navy, largely due to the fleet being more susceptible to unrest. In 1806 William Windham, then Secretary of State for War and Colonies, proposed significant reforms of the system utilized by the army. If fully implemented these reforms would have dramatically improved the status of the regular army as a possible career. Windham recognized that for a career in the army to become viable, there was a need to improve pay and, most importantly, increase pensions. Following Windham's reforms every soldier was to receive a pension and in an effort to make some postings more acceptable, two years served in the West Indies were to count as three served elsewhere. Widows' payments were not increased by Windham, although they were raised in 1812.

Rank	Pension	Rank	Pension
Colonel	£50	Ensign,	
Major	£30	Adjutant,	
Captain	£26	Chaplain,	£16
Lieutenant	£20	Surgeons	

Fig.10: Annual pensions received by widows, c1796.[77]

Windham's crucial pension reform was to ensure that they were available to every soldier, along with the widows, children, siblings and even the next of kin of those who died in service. To claim a pension a widow needed to take an oath and produce a certificate signed by an appropriate regimental colonel.[78]

Many of the pension reforms introduced by Windham would not benefit soldiers until later in the century. Sergeant Robert Edwards of the Wiltshire Militia was an example of an individual who entered the army during the Napoleonic Wars and did not receive such payments until 1834. Edwards enlisted in the militia in 1802, aged 28, serving for 30 years and 1 month. Due to a condition described by doctors as 'mental imbecility' he became an outpatient of Chelsea Hospital at the age of 60. His annual pension was £17 6s 8¾d, paid at quarterly intervals. To collect his pension Edwards, like all other pensioners, was required to prove his identity by producing two certificates signed by local magistrates. Impersonating a Chelsea out-patient was an offence punishable by hanging until 1818. There were several ways in which a pensioner could have forfeited his pension, including refusal to serve again after less than twenty-four years in the cavalry or twenty-one years in the infantry; failing to claim in four successive quarters; fraud; and 'violence or outrage towards persons employed in paying the pensioners'. Payments received in 'countries not forming part of His Majesty's dominions' were possible. A soldier could, for example, retire to Canada and still receive his pension.[79]

Prospects for claiming a pension were relatively good for soldiers as they had access to medical provision. Facilities were often rudimentary and unsanitary but they were regulated, and, in theory at least, staffed by trained personnel with access to 'up-to-date' advances in medicine. Overall responsibility for medical services lay with the medical board. This body consisted of the Surgeon General, Physician General, Inspector-General of Hospitals and a number of advisors. The advice of the Medical Board led to the army adopting some of the most up to date medical practices available in the early nineteenth century. In particular the army was at the forefront of inoculation and while soldiers were not necessarily inoculated as a matter of routine, the army invested considerable resources on the practice. In March 1801 the army spent £115 inoculating slave labourers in Jamaica. Inoculation was one of the few fields in which the army did not lag significantly behind the Royal Navy, widespread inoculation not being introduced for sailors until 1798. [80]

Despite being the amongst the 'best' available, those who advised the board were hampered by the limits of medical understanding and a conservative nature. This was a view expressed by Thomas Chevalier, a surgeon of some note who not only served as Surgeon to the Prince of Wales but also wrote a treatise on the treatment of musket wounds that was adopted by both the Irish and London Royal Colleges of Surgeons. In particular he urged a more modern approach be adopted towards amputation, a practice limited in the Prussian army from the mid-eighteenth century but one that remained common in the British army.[81]

The day-to-day running of medical services in the army was the responsibility of the Medical Departments. One such department existed for each of the army's two branches (Horse Guards and the Ordnance). At the head of the Horse Guards Medical Department was a director-general and two principal inspectors, both of who were qualified doctors. In 1812 the total number of staff employed in army hospitals were as follows: twenty-four physicians, one hundred and eighteen surgeons, ten assistant surgeons, five purveyors, twenty-five deputy purveyors and fifteen apothecaries. Hardly a massive number considering the size of the army. A feature of medical staff was the relatively large number of servants allocated. Physicians, surgeons, apothecaries, purveyors and some hospital mates each had a servant assigned, while inspectors were each allotted two. Funding for these servants was only to be received if they were recruited from amongst the local population. This arrangement placated medical personnel who wished to have servants but prevented the employment of soldiers, which was to prove a contentious issue in the army.[82]

Surgeons comprised almost half the personnel of medical departments and were perhaps the most important medical personnel. The status of surgeons in the army was ambiguous and somewhat similar to that of commissaries. Surgeons wore a uniform (that of the infantry but with a black plume) and held a commission, but were not combat soldiers. Despite on occasion serving in hospitals that were within earshot of battle, it was not anticipated that surgeons would become involved in combat. This was demonstrated by the case of Surgeon Shakelton. Shakelton was refused compensation for a wound received because, as a surgeon, he was not expected to be in the line of fire. That this was despite the wound being caused by a stray bullet some distance from the battle! Despite such instances it would be incorrect to assume that the army failed to acknowledge the contribution of surgeons to the war effort and the sacrifices they could make. The widow of Surgeon Dr. William Irvine, who died of a fever contracted whilst treating prisoners of war received £60 in compensation for her husband's death as it was considered to have been in the line of duty. Except for those employed as veterinaries (which was in any case a separate department), all army surgeons were expected to hold an appropriate qualification. Many felt undervalued by the army. As a result in 1804 a group serving in the Irish Militia petitioned the Duke of York for an increase in pay and improved chances for promotion.[83]

The daily running of hospitals effectively rested not with surgeons but the sergeants allocated to each ward. Possessing at best a rudimentary knowledge of medicine, these individuals were expected to fulfil a variety of duties within hospitals on a daily basis. Duties included ensuring rooms were ventilated and cleaned, that 'no man able to sit up is to lie upon his bed during the day', taking responsibility for patients' possessions, washing patients, and administering medicine.[84]

The medical system in the British army was not robust and could be overwhelmed by a large number of casualties. This problem was not only confined to war zones but also occurred in Britain itself. This was demonstrated during the Walcheren operation, which saw wounded conveyed directly from the war zone to hospitals in southern and eastern Britain. Such was the overcrowding many soldiers with fever with placed in local homes and understandably on occasion turned away by the occupants. Medical services were again overwhelmed during the opening phases of the Peninsula War, when the required infrastructure to handle large numbers of casualties was not in place locally. Hospitals were prepared to cope with the sick and, occasionally, wounded soldiers encountered in a garrison, not battlefield casualties. This resulted in medical students being sent into the hospitals at times of crisis. This proved popular with trainees, giving not only practice on live patients but also the dead. Cadavers in London cost no less than 3 guineas towards the end of the wars.[85]

When a soldier was injured on the battlefield the first stage of his treatment was conveyance to a medical post or field hospital. The process of transporting wounded away from the field of battle was beset with difficulties. Essential for the rapid removal of wounded was the provision of sufficient transport but this was not always achieved. The small number of wagons available to remove wounded after a battle was noted by the Duke of Wellington. He believed that the cause of the problem was not a poor allocation of wagons but rather the utilization of those allocated to transport items such as regimental account books. As a result general orders were issued restricting the practice. This no doubt horrified army accountants and had little real impact due to the scarcity of wagons.[86]

The break down in discipline that followed major battles further hindered the evacuation of wounded. Looting would invariably follow victory, while in the aftermath of a defeat the wounded would be left to fend for themselves as the army left the field. Those taken prisoner were fortunate as they were spared the fate of many of the injured. Countless wounded would fall victim to looters, succumb to their injuries or die of exposure as they lay on the battlefield.

Immediately after a battle swarms of looters would descend, primarily locals but also soldiers and their wives. Of the latter it was noted that they were particularly vicious looters:

They covered in number the ground of the field of battle when the action was over, and were seen stripping and plundering friend and foe alike. It is not doubted that they gave the finishing blow, to many an officer who was struggling with a mortal wound; Major Offley of the 23rd Regiment, who lay on the ground, unable to move, but not dead, is said to have fallen victim to this unheard of barbarity

After this looting the majority of dead bodies were left to simply decompose and following a battle the dead were often left on the field in great numbers. It was not uncommon to see unburied corpses weeks or months after an engagement. The aftermath of Salamanca was particularly grim as bodies decomposed in the heat. Barely a generation later British soldiers would cite the failure to bury the dead of either side after a battle as a characteristic of so called 'primitive' cultures such as the Zulu.[87]

A wounded soldier fortunate enough to be conveyed away from the battlefield had to await treatment in a field hospital. Frequently this was a makeshift establishment in a hastily acquired local building such as a farmhouse or barn. Such was the case after Waterloo and there could be large numbers of casualties would result in a backlog that could take days to clear. Inevitably many died of their wounds.

Perhaps the only positive in such circumstances was that there was little respect of rank regarding the treatment of the wounded in hospital: it was first come, first served.

There was a failure by the army to adequately supply hospitals with basic medicines and equipment to handle the aftermath of battles. The Duke of Wellington complained to Lord Castlereagh that even the relatively small battle of Talavera in 1809 seriously depleted hospital stores. Perhaps the most significant difficulty facing surgeons was that one of the most common wounds were those inflicted by musket balls. This was unfortunate as musket balls were capable of inflicting horrific and potentially life-threatening injuries. Of such injuries Thomas Chevalier, writing to the royal College of Surgeons, noted that:

a wound of this description must… produce more or less contusion and laceration of the wounded parts; will often be accompanied with hemorrhage; the fracture of a bone; and, in many instances, with the lodgment of extraneous substances.

Frequently the velocity of gunshots was sufficient to allow a musket ball to strip muscle from bone after entering the body, further adding to the trauma caused by the injury.[88]

Amazingly even the most severe damage inflicted by gunshots could be survived. In 1813 a soldier survived being shot through both his nose and the roof of his mouth. This is remarkable considering that the accepted medical practice in regard to gunshot wounds was, quite literally, hit and miss. In his treatise Chevalier urged surgeons to open wounds prior to operating. This was because such practice was perceived to be safer than 'making a random plunge, which may include parts that had better be avoided, and perhaps even miss the vessel it was intended to secure'. The advice contained within Chevalier's work was a step forwards. Thus, the Royal Colleges of Surgeons adopted Chevalier's treatise in 1806 but until this information was disseminated to surgeons the wounded continued to suffer the 'random plunge' of medical instruments.[89]

After leaving the field hospital the casualty could return straight to his unit, begin a period of convalescence or be sent to a permanent hospital some way from the front lines. If transferred to another hospital those able to walk made their journey on foot while the others were conveyed in wagons or upon mules. Compared to the situation regarding transport assigned to remove casualties, transportation for those moving between hospitals was relatively well organized. A wagon would be assigned to transport the packs of the wounded, while mules were allotted to carry either specified personnel or medicine. A column of such troops was placed in the charge of either a surgeon or an assistant surgeon and given rations for the required number of days, pre-cooked if possible. Containing large numbers of personnel and slow moving, these columns frequently caused heavy congestion on routes used for the transport of supplies and other military purposes.

Some personnel did not survive these journeys and of casualties arriving at Harwhich in 1809 it was noted that 'several [officers] have died and the men were buried by dozens... the landing at Harwich was truly an awful sight, several men died in the landing on the beach'. For those that did survive the eventual destinations varied. Convalescing personnel generally remained at the rear of the army, although officers could be allowed to return home. In such cases the period of absence was strictly defined and contact was to be made with the appropriate headquarters as soon as it ended. For the remaining sick and wounded the likely destination would have been either a permanent hospital or hospital ship, either of which could have been in the same region as their posting or Britain.[90]

Twenty-six hospital ships were active during the course of the Napoleonic and Revolutionary Wars, with the highest number active in a single year being nine in 1799. The navy had used hospital ships since Tudor times but inevitably the army lagged behind. Initially such vessels were viewed as being transports for the sick and wounded but from 1808 use was made of them as floating hospitals. Prior to this soldiers had been treated aboard similar vessels in colonies, such as HMS Seraphis in Jamaica, where shore based medical facilities were limited. Some craft were designated as stationary hospital ships and permanently moored at a single location. Hospital ships were often no more than regular naval or merchant vessels, converted through the addition of extra bedding, and often retained a secondary role as store ships (such has HMS Magnificent). Bad weather could make visits from shore impossible while they were described as being cramped, dirty and airless.[91]

Those soldiers sent to a regimental hospital were in theory better off than their comrades afloat. Regimental hospitals were governed by numerous regulations concerning ventilation, hygiene and diet. Each man was to be allocated a bed, the linen of which was to be changed fortnightly, and 5 feet of space. In practice hospital overcrowding, particularly following a large battle or in regions prone to high rates of sickness prevented such luxuries. At times the only available bedding was straw on the floor and space, especially in the wards of the West Indies, could be as little as 22 inches between patients.[92]

Military hospitals were not only filled with the wounded as soldiers could find themselves requiring medical attention for a variety of reasons. In such instances admittance to hospital was achieved through presentation of a certificate. Applications for these were made through the office of the

Adjutant-General or, in the case of Commissariat personnel, the Commissary General. These applications were assessed by medical boards, which met at selected hospitals on the fifth, twelfth and twentieth days of each month. A period spent in hospital was governed by strict regulations that were to be posted in each hospital and read out to new patients. A hospital uniform was issued that consisted of white long coat, flannel waist coat, shirt, trousers and a cap. Entry to hospitals was strictly controlled so visits from colleagues were rare, as were some of the comforts usually enjoyed by soldiers in the field. To ensure these rules were adhered to sentinels were appointed:

> to prevent all persons from entering the hospital, the staff, or officers in uniform, patients and servants of the hospital excepted; to be particularly careful in preventing liquor, or anything improper from being carried into the hospital. No patients to be allowed to go out without a ticket of leave from the surgeon.

Ward sergeants were responsible for imposing further restrictions and were instructed to 'prevent patients from spitting on the floor, irregularities, gaming [and] swearing', as well as preventing the defacing of hospital property. In addition to these restrictions normal military conventions, such as morning roll call, continued to be applied. For all of this a soldier enjoyed a deduction of 9d per day from his wages.[93]

After several weeks or months in hospital patients would be either sent back to their units or allowed a period of convalescing. Some were granted permission to return home for the period of convalescence. While popular with those concerned it was less so with senior army officers. The Duke of Wellington in particular was known to be critical of the policy allowing troops to return to Britain and it was observed by a junior officer that 'Lord Wellington is very adverse to sparing a man; and the two words "return home" puts him into a fury'. This was unsurprising when it is considered that many supposedly 'convalescing' officers took the opportunity to indulge in the night life of Lisbon. As a result regulations were introduced to curb the practice but met with mixed success.[94]

Convalescing was a privilege reserved in the main for officers. Private Green of the 68th Regiment of Foot was typical of soldiers allowed to recover by being given light duties. Billeted in a makeshift prefabricated hut along with fellow convalescing soldiers, he spent his time sweeping the streets of Lisbon until considered able to return to his regiment. Even more common than the light duties in which Green was engaged while convalescing was an immediate return to the soldier's unit. This policy was popular with senior officers as it released manpower but frequently troops returned to active duty too early, a situation which brought with it implications for their health.[95]

Admittance to hospital for treatment of various ailments was an advantage enjoyed by soldiers over civilians because, despite their failings, military establishments were relatively well regulated and, while not free, incurred only a minor cost. Despite these advantages disease and rigours of service took a toll on many soldiers. On 31st May 1808 Captain Jennings of the 28th Regiment made his decision to retire from the army, stating that:

at this time my health having suffered considerably and finding myself no longer fit to encounter the hardship of actual service I resolve to retire… after eighteen years service chiefly foreign in which period I completed several hard campaigns without ever having experienced any wounds or other corporal injury, the usual consequence of field service.

During service Jennings had suffered from an occasional liver complaint, in addition to 'violent and alarming' bleeding from his head towards the end of his career. Despite this Jennings regarded himself as fortunate not to have sustained any wounds. Jennings may have avoided the fiercest fighting of the Napoleonic Wars but his experiences demonstrate how a soldier's health could suffer despite avoiding the trauma of injury on the battlefield.[96]

Death was an inevitable feature of life in the army. Many soldiers doubted they would survive time in hospital and in such situations turned to religion for comfort. Such soldiers could be disappointed as chaplains could be notable by their absence. This was despite the fact that the army had a commitment to provide chaplains, and associated facilities, to enable religious observance amongst its troops. The organization responsible for providing soldiers with access to religion was the Chaplain General's Department, the personnel of which operated at divisional level. Chaplains were exclusively Anglican in this period, and it was not until much later in the nineteenth century that those from other denominations of Christianity were introduced. For the army religion was a potentially difficult subject. There were those in Britain who saw the army as a bulwark of a protestant state, its commander in chief the son of the head of the Church of England. For the army religion was only a significant issue when it threatened discipline. [97]

In early nineteenth century Britain Dissenters (non-protestant Christians) were actively discriminated against. Catholics were perceived as loyal to the pope whilst Methodism seemed opposed to hierarchy. In the army such individuals were prevented them from being promoted above the rank of Captain. It was a farcical situation that reflects the stupidity of prejudice. If a Catholic had suspect loyalty due to their faith, why allow them into the army let alone command a company? More to the point, the army happily operated alongside allies commanded by Catholic generals. Besides being founded upon misunderstanding other denominations, the system ignored the fact that the protestant faith was no more or less disruptive to the military than Catholicism.

An example of a serious conflict between religious beliefs and military duty arose in 1808 on the island of Jersey. One Private Philip Arthurs of the militia was 'imprisoned in the goal of St. Helens for refusing to attend the regimental drills and military reviews on Sundays, from scruples of conscience and praying belief'. Arthurs was a practicing Anglican, not a Catholic, Methodist or of any other so called 'dissenting faith'. Arthurs appealed against his imprisonment, stating that he would be willing to attend on a weekday. The military authorities stated that allowing the militia to choose their own day of drill would undermine discipline. Ultimately the Privy Council dismissed the appeal, not on grounds of military necessity but that Sunday morning drill was the least disruptive for those employed as labourers, farmers and fishermen. The needs of the military and the Church all took second place to economics in early nineteenth century Britain.[98]

The religious views of soldiers did not always result in imprisonment but could still result in overt opposition to military practices. While serving on a court martial in 1813 George Hennell wrote that he disproved of the system because 'I am accountable to a superior tribunal whose judge has said "Blessed are the merciful for they shall obtain mercy"'. Another soldier whose views were shaped by his religious beliefs was Quarter Master William Surtees. Surtees served with the Rifle Brigade and underwent a profound religious conversion while serving in Spain. After this he became highly critical of his fellow officers. Soldiers who sought to convert their comrades to their views often met with abuse and even threats of violence, as discovered by the anonymous author of *Life in the 38th Foot* who admitted his constant preaching made him unpopular.[99]

The army's actual policy towards religion can at best be described as lethargic. This was apparent at the most basic level, specifically the allocation of chaplains to each division. While divisional chaplains were in theory present in regular formations, there was no such provision in the auxiliary formations. This was caused by the structure of militia, volunteer and fencible units, formations that were often administered outside of a divisional structure and thus unable to benefit from the existence of associated personnel. In consequence chaplains were assigned to certain auxiliary formations, but were rarely on the active strength of such units.

By failing to fully integrate chaplains into the structure of auxiliary formations, the effectiveness of such individuals could have been undermined by lack of familiarity with those under their care. In part this could have been avoided due to the nature of auxiliary units, which tended to be drawn from a single locality, but it is possible that such a chaplain would have known few individuals originating from outside of his own parish. Even chaplains in regular formations failed to make close bonds with troops in regular formations. This included even Surtees, who's painful religious conversation evidently occurred with little input from military clergy. Above all the army's policy towards chaplains in the auxiliary forces demonstrated that there was relatively little concern about the religious practices of British soldiers. In consequence only a limited effort was made to force the Anglican faith upon them.

On active service chaplains were expected to conduct church services twice per week and divine service each Sunday. For such services chaplains were instructed that 'more men shall not be assembled for that purpose [a church service] at a time, than the voice can reach, a precaution very necessary to ensure the attention of the soldier... [to allow this] the chaplain shall perform the service successively to the different corps of his division'. The preferred location for such services was the open air as there was invariably sufficient space under cover. Due to a variety of factors, services occurred significantly less frequently than was recommended. Private Wheeler noted that 'in winter quarters [chaplains] once on a Sunday (weather permitting), perform divine service, but when the campaign opens, it is seldom, or ever, an opportunity offers'. Thus weather and the practicalities of military life could prevent religious observance. Many battles – including Waterloo - were fought on Sundays, limiting the time available for religious observance.[100]

Sundays were frequently perceived by soldiers on campaign to be like any other day. This was a significant departure from attitudes in civilian life as both pressure from ecclesiastical authorities and state regulations restricted the activities that could occur. Non-religious meetings, for example, could not be held on Sundays by civilians following the Sunday Observance Act (1781) and Seditious Meeting Act (1795). In 1811 the Adjutant-General recommended that services should 'close with a short practical sermon, suited to the habits and understanding of soldiers'. This reflected a realization that existing religious sermons were not seen as relevant by many soldiers. Conversely demand for religious services remained high, over stretching the limited number of chaplains in the army, even when multiple sermons were delivered on a Sunday. Lieutenant Bingham complained that the small number of chaplains available was barely sufficient to do more than 'remind us that we are Protestants', while it seems a number of soldiers wished to attend services but could not do so due to a lack of chaplains. There is little evidence that this was due to failing to meet recruitment targets. At the very least the army was under concerned it was not. Rather the regulation number of Chaplains was insufficient to meet demand.[101]

When units were deployed in European countries the pressure on chaplains was in part relieved through the utilization of local facilities by the troops. Catholic soldiers in Spain had used churches of their own religion while on occasion soldiers proved willing to use other denominations' places of worship. The Protestant Private Green stated that he attended both 'churches and dissenting chapels' while in Ireland. This says much about soldiers such as Green, who rose above contemporary prejudice. It also brings into doubt how widespread anti-dissenter sentiment was in the general population.[102]

While many overseas garrisons possessed a sound supporting infrastructure of stores, hospitals and regimental schools, the same could not be said of the provision of religious facilities and Chaplains. This changed in the post war period as the army shifted its focus from Europe to the growing Empire. From 1812 to 1815 the only overseas garrison to have a chaplain assigned to it for any length of time had been Honduras (a Chaplain J. Armstrong). Between 1816 and 1820, however, there was to be a marked and steady growth in both the number of chaplains and the overseas garrisons to which they were deployed. Of particular note is that besides serving an increased number of garrisons, in most years the number of chaplains actually exceeded the number of garrisons. This demonstrated chaplains were available to serve the more dispersed detachments. By far the greatest concentration of Chaplains serving outside of Europe in the post-war period was in the Caribbean region.

	Year				
	1816	1817	1818	1819	1820
Number of Chaplains	6	14	19	18	29
Number of garrisons served	2	8	8	19	19

Figure 11: Chaplains serving in overseas garrisons, 1816 – 20.[103]

Of the 14 Chaplain's serving overseas at the start of 1817, 13 were in the Caribbean. By 1820 chaplains were to be found with garrisons such as those in New South Wales, Cape Colony and West Africa. A consequence of these deployments was a dramatic increase in the wage bill for chaplains serving outside of Europe. In 1815 this had amounted to only 7s a month, which was paid to Chaplain J. Armstrong in Honduras. By 1816 this bill had risen to £120 2s 7d, while by 1820, it stood at £416 13s 4d per month.

Despite holding the equivalent of major's rank, there existed considerable variation in Chaplains' pay. In the Caribbean during 1817 there existed six different rates of pay. This ranges from 2s3d to 14s 3d per week. This pay structure remained relatively unaltered until 1819, when an additional rate of pay (16s per week) was introduced for the senior chaplain on Jamaica in 1819. Unusually wages increased or decreased according to posting.[104]

---

[69] Gurwood (ed), *Despatches and General Orders*, p.348.
[70] H. Torrens to Duke of Wellington, Horse Guards, 5th November 1811, NAM 6807/221, pp.40-1.
[71] Half Yearly Report on 25th Light Dragoons, Bagalore, 15th February 1813, NAM 6112/78, p.184.
[72] Gurwood (ed), *General Orders*, p.32.
[73] Letter from War Office to Regimental Colonels, 19th July 1811, PRO ADM 201/20, Discharges, Pay, Pensions and Allowances (Royal Marines); Gurwood (ed), *General Orders*, pp.323-4; Illegible to Lord Bathurst, Paris, 19th March 1816, PRO WO 28/14, Letters from Quarter Master General's Department, 1816 January to June;
[74] J. MacDonald, *Instructions for the Conduct of Infantry in Actual Service* (London, Egerton, 1807), p.cl.
[75] NAM 6112/78, p155.
[76] Duke of York to Viscount Palmerston, Horse Guards, 26th August 1811. As ever the Royal Navy was even further head, having established a similar institution in 1729.
[77] Anon, *A Treatise on Military Finance* (Whitehall, Egerton, 1796),p.96.
[78] PRO WO 25/3995, Register of Annual Bounty Paid to Deceased Officers Widows; PRO WO 245/134, W. Horton to Deputy Treasurer of ChelseaHospital, Glasgow, 1816.
[79] Affidavit of Magistrate, WSRO 632/134, Certificate(s) of Sergeant R. Edwards, Out Patient of Chelsea Hospital, 1834
[80] Royal College of Physicians to Privy Council, 5th February 1805; Instructions to the Board of Health, 13th February 1805, PRO PC 1/3643; NAM 7508/55/2, Particular Account Number 2. Being for Monies Paid and Advanced by Matthew Atkinson, Agent General.
[81] T. Chevalier, *A Treatise on Gunshot Wounds* (London, Bagster, 1806), pp.104-122
[82] Army List, 1812 (London, War Office, 1812); Quinto de Banos, 8th July 1811, NAM 6807/221, pp.14-18; In 1811 orders were issued demanding that soldiers of the Peninsula army employed as servants without authorization be returned to their units as the use of soldiers in this role was having a detrimental impact on manpower.

[83] Sometimes referred to as Shekelton. PRO WO 43/366, Wound gratuity refused to army surgeon Robert Shakelton; PRO WO 25/3995; NAM 6801/43, Letter from Irish Militia Surgeons to the Duke of York Expressing Concerns about Pay, c1804

[84] NAM 6807/370/29, Orders For Regimental Hospitals, 1804.

[85] Dent to his Mother, Colchester, 5th March 1809, NAM 7008/11/2.

[86] Gurwood (ed), *General Orders*, p.49.

[87] Buckley, *The Napoleonic War Journal of Captain Thomas Henry Browne*, p174.

[88] Wellington to Castlereagh, Talavera, 21st August 1809, PRO WO 1/228; Chevalier, *A Treatise on Gunshot Wounds*, p.2.

[89] Bingham to his mother, nr Echelar, 3rd April 1813, NAM 6807/163, p.59; Chevalier, *A Treatise on Gunshot Wounds*, p.75.

[90] Dent to Mother, Colchester, 12th September 1809, NAM 7008/11/2; Standing Orders, Order No. 52, NAM 6807/221, p.11.

[91] Secretary of Customs, Extract on the Report on the Collector and Comptroller of the Customs at Sciliy Relative to the Stationary Hospital Ships', 2nd February 1805, PRO PC 1/3643; PRO ADM 102/1, Hospital Ship Musters; Lieutenant Colonel J. H. Plumridge, *Hospital Ships and Ambulance Trains* (London, Seeley, 1975), pp.16-26.

[92] *Statistical Report on the Sickness Mortality and Invaliding Among the Troops of the West Indies* (London, HMSO, 1838), p.4.

[93] NAM 6807/221, Standing Orders, Orders No. 51 and 52, p.11.

[94] Burgos 3/10/12, NAM 6807/163

[95] J. Green, *The Vicissitudes of a Soldier's Life* (Cambridge, Ken Trotman, 1996), pp.201-202.

[96] NAM 8301/102, Memoirs of Captain Peter Jennings, pp.133-4.

[97] Adjutant General Harry Calvert to Duke of Wellington, Horse Guards, 8th November 1811, NAM 6807/221, pp.39-40.

[98] PRO PC 1/3866, Petition Brought by Philip Arthurs, Private of the South West Regiment of the Jersey militia, 11th April 1809; Response of John de Veulle Griffith, Jersey, 16th August 1809.

[99] M. Glover (ed), *A Gentleman Volunteer: The Letters of George Hennell From the Peninsular War 1812-13* (London, Heinemann, 1979), p.113; W. Surtees, *Twenty Five Years in the Rifle Brigade* (London, Greenhill, 1996), p.314; NAM 7912/21, pp.33-34.

[100] Adjutant General Harry Calvert to Duke of Wellington, Horse Guards, 8th November 1811, NAM 6807/22, pp.39-40; Brackets in original. Liddell – Hart (ed), *The Letters of Private Wheeler*, p.153; Glover (ed), *A Gentleman Volunteer*, p.201.

[101] Bingham to his mother, Galispendo 6th March 1813, NAM 6807/163, p.12.

[102] Green, *Vicissitudes*, p.218.

[103] 'Particular sums Ordered in Repayment of Advances Made by the Commissariat Department Abroad, on Account of the Pay of Officiating Chaplains 1817 to 1820', PRO WRO 25/254.

[104] 1817, Warrant Numbers 2777; 2886; 1819, Warrant Numbers 2802; 2804, PRO WRO 25/254.

CHAPTER 6
Counties versus Napoleon

Nothing scared the British political establishment more than an invasion by Revolutionary France. It was fear that such an event would result in anarchy, uprising and rampant equality across the land. To those of a conservative mind set the Devil had may as well have appeared (the form of which Bonaparte took in many a pamphlet of the time). That the ruling elite were so paranoid of unrest but unwilling to improve life for many Britons suggests a somewhat confused way of thinking. Whether there was a real threat of invasion was irrelevant. The population and government believed it be imminent. The more realistic threat of insurrection added to the urgency.

In a rare show of common sense the government recognized the importance of supply and logistics in anti-invasion planning. Besides troop movements and building projects a key element was a document entitled 'Proposals for Rendering the Body of the People Instrumental in the General Defence'. The document placed much emphasis on the protection of property during invasion. An announcement by the Lord Lieutenant of Hampshire stated the plans were intended to guarantee 'the particular protection and security of persons and property of the inhabitants of this country... and the indemnifying persons who may suffer in their property by such measures for that purpose'. Despite such noble sentiments the protection of property was only a minor concern. The real aim was to find what supplies were available and guarantee their distribution.[105]

The process begun in 1803 when questionnaires were distributed to each county under the Defense of the Realm Act. The whole plan depended on the structures of county government: parishes would report to subdivisions, in turn these would report back to the Deputy Lords Lieutenant. It was to be the Lords Lieutenant who had ultimate responsibility for a county's invasion preparations. With an invasion seemingly imminent a tight schedule was imposed, with reports from parishes expected to be received within a month of instructions being issued.

County officials such as magistrates were to help support a county's efforts in the event of an invasion but this posed a problem. These same individuals often held commissions in forces such as the militia, and could be called away from the county to fight the French at the very moment they were needed to prepare the county for an invasion. To limit the impact of such persons being called away the Lords Lieutenant were advised that 'it is essential that the [relevant officials] should if possible be persons not holding commissions as volunteer officers, nor liable on any other account to be called away from the county'. The number of individuals who had roles in both the auxiliary forces and county government were considerable. In Wiltshire the commander of the militia, Colonel Henry Herbert, Earl of Caernarvon (sic), was also a Deputy Lieutenant, an office that entailed separate duties in the event of invasion.[106]

The preparations undertaken by each county were to be based on a series of reports from each parish, the most important of which were designated schedules one through to nine. Fully completed the schedules would have amounted to a miniature doomsday book of England during the years 1803 to 1804. Schedule 1 was concerned with available manpower, those unfit for service (labelled 'infirm'), the number of aliens and the number of Quakers. The Quakers were singled out due to their pacifist beliefs. That Protestant bigotry didn't single out Catholics as an unreliable horde of anarchist cut throats supporting a French invader is somewhat surprising considering certain policies. Similarly Methodists also escaped suspicion in the survey.[107]

A killing a day

Schedule 1	Available Manpower
Schedule 2	Food
Schedule 3	Overseers
Schedule 4	Men willing to arm themselves
Schedule 5	Men willing to act as labourers
Schedule 6	Men willing to carry supplies
Schedule 7	Millers willing to mill flour
Schedule 8	Bakers
Schedule 9	Waterborne transport

Figure 12: Preparations for invasion, schedules one to nine.

Schedule 2 was a survey of available livestock and 'deadstock', otherwise known as crops. This encompassed the following categories: numbers of oxen, cows, young cattle and colts, sheep and goats, pigs, riding and draft horses, wagons and carts; quarters of wheat, oats, barley, beans and peas, potatoes and malt; loads of straw and hay; while flour 'and other meal' was given special attention with counts of both quarts and sacks. Schedules 7 and 8 built on this by listing millers and bakers who promised to supply goods in the event of an invasion.

Schedule 6 revealed the number of wagons.

Details included the number of draught animals they required, the parish that they would supply and details of drivers. Emphasis was to be placed upon four-horse wagons, such vehicles seen as sufficient to carry either fifty hundredweight of flour, grain, wood or coal, or twenty hundredweight of bread, biscuit or straw. The vehicles recorded in schedule 6 were to be supplemented by those described in schedule 9. This sought to determine the waterborne transport available in a parish. Throughout these plans the role of the transport was to be the movement of supplies, rather than other tasks such as evacuation of wounded personnel. This lack of consideration for medical purposes was to be one of the most glaring deficiencies amongst the plans established in 1803. Such was the extent of the investigation into what each parish possessed it should have been a relatively simple task to add possible sites for infirmaries to the list.

Schedule 3 was particularly important as it determined who in the parish would be overseers for the various items outlined in other schedules. These individuals were to be responsible for implementing the key component of a county's invasion preparations. This was to be nothing less than the uprooting of whole communities in the path of an advancing enemy army. The purpose of listing the infirm in schedule 1 was to ensure means to remove them had been arranged prior to invasion and an overseer was also appointed for this task. Livestock, wagons, money and account books were all to be moved with the population.

The government was guilty of excessive optimism on a number of levels. The first is was the evident belief that the evacuation of whole communities would take place in orderly manner. Second was the idea that the population would need prompting to move. By 1803 the population had consumed a decade's worth of propaganda about revolutionaries intent on murder, pillage and general anarchy. It's unlikely any civilian would have willingly remained at home around to see this in practice.

To hinder the enemy's efforts to live off the land, bakers and millers were instructed how best to render their equipment unusable by an invader. This was to be achieved by breaking the crowns of ovens and upper mill stones respectively. Such destruction was evidence of a policy designed to prevent resources from falling into enemy hands as much as it was a means of civil defense. Although a common practice in response to any invasion great importance was attached to denying the French invader resources. Due to the Royal Navy it was envisaged that the enemy would be forced to exist solely on supplies drawn from their locality.[108]

By its nature the plan had to prepare for a number of contingencies, a French advance inland being one of them. This was not the sole reason for the continued evacuation of communities in the event of invasion. The priority was maximizing the availability of supplies to defending forces. Fully implemented, the invasion preparations were to have enabled the army to utilize the resources not only of the counties targeted by invasion but also those adjacent or further from the enemy lodgment. For the duration of the invasion at least the army would be given free rein to requisition the resources it required to drive the French back into the sea. As for the resources not required by the army, some would have been removed but the rest sacrificed for national defense.

This was of course Britain in 1803 so even with the nation staring at catastrophe the rights of private ownership had to be seen to be protected. The requirement to move ledgers proved that even if faced with invasion the government maintained one eye on the cash box. Orders were issued to county lieutenants stating that 'the first principle is an indemnification from the communities at large... for the value of all stock which may be removed in consequence of invasion'. In this respect, it appeared that the policy was little different to that which already existed regarding procurement and operated by organizations such as the Commissariat. It was when the practice is considered in the overall context of the anti-invasion scheme that the assault on the rights of ownership becomes apparent.

Livestock would have effectively ceased to be the property of the owner, despite instructions to brand each animal with the mark of the parish before moving them. In many cases creating such a mark was one of the first acts in implementing the planning. Livestock were to be effectively little more than a mobile source of food for the army under the supervision of selected citizens (specifically the overseers named in schedule 3). Orders to the overseers of the livestock from each parish regarding ownership were only a façade, as the livestock would have effectively been placed under army control at the moment of evacuation. Once livestock and other supplies arrived at a depot or market it would be purchased by commissaries and receipts issued. Significantly, even if goods were not purchased owners required permission from a commissary to sell them. Once purchased by a commissary the normal procedures of the army would have came into effect and the items would have eventually filtered through the various stages of the logistics system until they reached the intended recipients.

The prices at which cattle and commodities such as flour were to be sold to the army were to be decided by magistrates. Evidently these prices would have been regularly assessed and considered, giving rise to the possibility of price fluctuations and varying prices between localities. This would have been a new way of operating for the army in Britain as it was normally maintained through long-term contracts that provided both low and stable prices.

While livestock were mobile, items too bulky to be moved to depots would have been required by the army. The village of Box in Somerset contained amongst other items 346 quarters of wheat, 63 quarters of oats and 1059 loads of hay, but only three wagons allocated to the task of moving these goods. The result was a plan to convert evacuated villages into supply depots. From them supplies such as grain and flour could be distributed. Such villages would have effectively became magazines, with the advantage that many already lay on a road and canal network.[109]

Parishes were instructed to appoint 'several and discreet trusty persons' for the task of remaining behind in the village after its evacuation. These individuals were allowed to leave only when the enemy approached or they were surrounded. How this latter situation was to be escaped was not made clear and it is possible many would have opted for discretion rather than valour at the first sight of a French column! A number of millers and bakers may have remained in the villages. Such individuals would have co-operated closely with the Commissariat, which would have both purchased the goods they produced and arranged the delivery of necessary supplies (such as flour for bakers if none was available locally).

Commissaries would have been required to advise civilians how best to bake their bread. It was the view of many civilian bakers that ovens could only be used to produce four batches of bread per day, although in the military six was standard practice. It was anticipated that yeast would be in particularly short supply and bakers were advised to produce either unleavened bread, or manufacture their own yeast. The latter was to be achieved through using a recipe written for the Dunbar garrison in 1796, rather than experimentation. It was the belief of the authorities that 'it is highly necessary to caution everyman concerned in supplying an army, against placing any confidence in schemes not perfectly and satisfactorily tried himself'. The optimum loaf size was to be between three to four and a half pounds, with a thick crust, as such bread stayed fresher longer. Guidance was also to be given how best to stack bread on wagons (preferably when cold) and the duration of any storage prior to its consumption. This advice is notable because similar written instructions to commissaries in foreign theatres of war do not appear to have existed.[110]

The scale of the task facing the county authorities when moving whole populations cannot be underestimated. Added to the mass movement of people, hundreds of cattle and thousands of sheep and goats would be moved. Preparations were required to sustain animals and humans alike. For livestock, orders advised that the route taken included pasture and water, while civilians ordered to leave their homes were advised to take with them salted or dried provisions. Only wagon drivers and associated personnel were to receive supplies from stores, rations consisting of one and a half pounds of bread per day for each man and either ten pounds of oats or fourteen pounds of hay per horse. This ration was comparable to that prescribed for horses in the Peninsula campaign.[111]

The movement of large numbers of civilians and livestock would have placed a heavy burden on the transport infrastructure. Lords Lieutenant were expected to arrange for civilians to follow routes away from the invasion area. These routes were not to be along roads allocated to the army. If unavoidable, such routes could only be used by civilians for as little time as possible. It is clear that the proposals were written with little regard to the reality of moving columns of panicked civilians. Perhaps a greater concern were the large herds of sheep present on the South Downs. Due to their proximity to the English Channel would likely have been removed soon after an invasion. This would have caused considerable disruption not only to the transport infrastructure but also to the regional economy.

The wagons allocated for the transport of supplies were to be ready to move within twenty fours notice. It was expected that they would travel twenty-five to thirty miles per day, depending on load. Such a figure may have been optimistic. These vehicles occupied an ambiguous position within the command structure and it is unclear whether they were to be given the same priorities on the roads as the military. This was crucial because if the vehicles were to be regarded as military, civilians were expected to give way, but if this was not the case wagons, and the supplies on them, would have been expected to travel cross-country as much as possible. Such vehicles had only limited cross-country mobility, a problem not satisfactorily rectified by the recommendation of carrying a shovel to aid cross country mobility.[112]

The rights of the individuals manning the wagons was made clear to them when opting for this duty. Each vehicle was to be given a certificate identifying the owner, driver, number of horses and, most significantly the date at which it was to be discharged from duty. Drivers were to be paid for each day of service, according to rates set by magistrates and lieutenants in each county (presuming these officials were not leading the militia on the frontline or, a distinct possibility, fleeing a French advance). Every wagon was to have a conductor of stores, responsible for ensuring receipts were received for all goods transferred and rations received. The system had the potential to be a disaster, with drivers unwilling to move without the appropriate paperwork or because their period of service had expired.[113]

Living off requisitioned cattle and its advance probably slowed by columns of refugees and evacuees, the British army would have sought to drive back the invader. The regular army would have been supported in this task not only by the militia but other formations created to resist invasion. A scheme to raise a corps of mounted scouts and guides from local populations was never implemented but new Volunteer units were to be raised. Besides infantry and cavalry formations, the Volunteers included pioneer corps that were to be raised from each parish. The pioneers were to have operated in companies of twenty-five to fifty men, commanded by a lieutenant or captain respectively (schedule 5). In the event that the minimum number of twenty-five could not be attained companies from different parishes would have been combined. Equipment would have varied between units as personnel were required to provide their own. The following was a recommended list of items for a unit of twenty-five men: six each of pickaxes, spades and shovels, three billhooks and four felling axes. In addition it was also noted that 'a proportion of wheelbarrows will also be very serviceable'.[114]

The ability of each parish to supply personnel for

the new formations was initially based on the number of individuals able to arm themselves. It was anticipated that each parish would be able to supply contingents of both cavalry and infantry. Cavalry were requested to supply a pistol or a sword (preferable both), while those on foot would provide either a 'firelock' (musket) or pitchfork. It was stated that a ratio of one musket between four men was initially sufficient. There was thus a very real possibility that volunteer units resisting a French invader in 1803 could expect to engage the French with a ratio of one musket to three other weapons.[115]

There was no attempt to emulate the tactics of Irish rebels in producing large numbers of pikes. Easily produced by village blacksmiths, these had proved to be effective weapons against cavalry in close terrain during the rebellion of 1798. Given the proven value of the pike in the hands of trained or willing civilians the failure to adopt the weapons for the volunteers appears inexplicable. Conservative military thinking no doubt influenced the decision but the most likely explanation is that, fearful of unrest, the government was reluctant to promote the manufacture of such a weapon in the English provinces.

Significant difficulties would have been

encountered in supplying the volunteer units due to the variety of firearms that would have been found in their ranks. As individuals were encouraged to supply their own firearms it is likely that everything from dueling pistols to fowling pieces, in a variety of calibers, would have been employed. As a result those supplying firearms were requested to also provide a bullet mold and powder horn 'lest the bore of their arms, being smaller than those of the army, should prevent their using the ammunition made up for the King's Troops'.[116]

The invasion had occurred, the army is deployed. What would happen next? Justices would have continued to supervise the passage of troops. In August 1804 regulations were published concerning 'the preservation of good order, to be adopted in case of invasion, in each county in Great Britain'. If these regulations had been implemented it is apparent that the civil power, while officially supported by the military, would have effectively become subordinated to its requirements. The regulations required that in the event of invasion magistrates would sit daily, along with an officer of the volunteers and chief superintendent of constables. The primary task of these bodies would have been suppressing disorder in the army's rear areas, guarding prisoners and providing escorts for convoys. Such duties could have only been fulfilled if the volunteers were present in the county. It is questionable if such formations would have turned out at all: many militiamen in Ireland opted to remain with their families when called upon to act against Irish rebels in 1798.

If deprived of a military force to deploy at the request of the army, magistrates would have been confined to determining the rates of pay for wagon drivers employed in support of the military, and the price at which items such as flour and bread were to be sold to commissaries. How long this situation existed would in part have been decided by the efforts of the British armed forces, aided by the invasion preparations implemented by the magistrates, Lord Lieutenants and parish officials of counties across Britain.

---

[105] *Salisbury Journal*, 11th July 1803, p.3.
[106] Circular from Lord Hawksbury, Whitehall, 20th August 1804, PRO WO 55/1548/17, Regulations for each county, in case of Invasion; WSRO A1/752/19, Return of the Qualifications of Deputy Lieutenants and Commissioned Officers [of Wiltshire Militia], 29th January 1796.
[107] WSRO 1719/30, Wiltshire Lieutenancy Papers Dealing with the Parish [of Box's] Preparation to Raise a Volunteer Force to Meet the Anticipated French Invasion, schedules 1 to 9; Voluntary Contributions, Anonymous pamphlet, 1798, WSRO 1719/30.
[108] General Meeting of the Lieutenancy, Sarum, 19th November 1803, WSRO 1719/30; PRO WO 30/141, Proposals for Rendering the Body

of the People Instrumental in the General Defence, saving their property, and distressing the enemy, by removing the means of subsistence, from threatened parts of the country. Published by authority, pp3, 5n.

[109] WSRO 1719/30, schedules 2 and 6; PRO WO 30/141, p.15.

[110] PRO WO 30/141, pp.5, 24-30.

[111] PRO WO 30/141, pp.4, 17; Orders, General Meeting of the Lieutenancy, Sarum, 19th November 1803, WSRO 1719/30.

[112] WSRO 1719/30, schedule 6.

[113] PRO WO 30/141, pp.16-17.

[114] Orders, General Meeting of the Lieutenancy, Sarum, 19th November 1803, WSRO 1719/30; PRO WO 30/141, p.6.

[115] To the Minister, Churchwardens, Overseers of the Poor, and Principal Inhabitants of Box in the County of Wilts, from the Lord Lieutenant, Wilton House, 2nd August 1803, WSRO 1719/30.

[116] WSRO 1719/30, schedule 4.

CHAPTER 7
Measuring success

The British army entered what would become the Napoleonic Wars at a low point. The loss of the American Revolution was still being felt and the start to the new conflict was hardly auspicious. The fiasco in Flanders was so bad that the Duke of Wellington later remarked it showed 'how not to do it'. By the time of the final defeat of Napoleon in 1815 the British army had found new confidence. This confidence was accompanied by an effective propaganda machine that triumphed the importance and success of British arms, British tactics and, as portrayed by some parties, the near magical abilities of a certain Duke of Wellington. The success was so complete, why change it? The Crimean War showed the folly of this but as late as the 1870s elements of British military thinking remained under the thrall of the victories of the early 1800s.

Unpicking the myth is important because it places the supply and maintenance of the army in context. Logistics is key to winning wars so understanding the success or otherwise of an army can be a gateway to understanding how effectively it was maintained. The British army was far from being the overwhelming success it may appear. It was not until 1808 that the army began to make a significant contribution to the conflict with France. Besides the Flanders debacle, there was the fiasco in South America that resulted in the capture of a force sent to Argentina, while closer to home the army initially struggled to contain the 1798 rebellion in Ireland. Perhaps its most direct contribution prior to 1808 had been thwarting French ambitions in Egypt. Indirectly the role of the army in safeguarding and expanding the Empire, to which the Egyptian adventure was linked, was arguably more significant.

After 1808 the role of the army in fighting France became more direct. Despite jingoistic sentiments, romanticizing the conflict and swashbuckling literary heroes such as Bernard Cornwell's Richard Sharpe, the main contribution of the British force in Spain and Portugal was tying down French forces. Spain may have been an ulcer but it was the advancing armies of Austria, Russia and Prussia that inflicted the killing blows. Looking elsewhere the army supported friendly regimes such as those in Italy, preventing French expansion, but again this alone could not win a war. The problem for the army in all of this was its size. Britain trailed behind the major powers in terms of troops it could field. In part this was due to the Royal Navy but also the nation's small size. Of the major European powers only Prussia and Spain had smaller populations. Financially and industrially, however, Britain led the field. It is this that leads to the key for appraising how effectively the British army was maintained.

A small army, supported by the leading economic and industrial power of the hemisphere (China's vast pool of manpower gave it a declining industrial lead at this time). It is irrefutable that Britain had the resources and finances for world leading logistics system. In some respects it was. The global reach of the system was unrivaled until the United States emerged as the dominant power in the mid twentieth century. The global reach of the British army is a lasting achievement that continues, albeit significantly reduced, into the twenty first century. It is a capability that is a bench mark for any appraisal of a modern British government's defense policy.

Ironically it was within the borders of Europe that the system seems to have fell apart the most. It was here that the army was tested against a peer opponent and at best performed only adequately. Soldiers serving in Spain and Portugal complained of hunger and dressed in tattered uniforms. These were basic requirements that the army failed to meet. The failure was not universal but it seems inconceivable how the soldiers of a cloth manufacturing nation could find themselves in such a severe situation. It was a situation not unique to the British army but cloth manufacture had helped drive the industrial revolution.

Severe shortages of key items may not have been the

norm, they were not unknown. Furthermore it is a near certainty that they were more widespread than believed. One benefit of the myth of the all-conquering British army was a thirst for knowledge of the conflict. The result was a deluge of memoirs, letter collections and diaries published by soldiers who served (many were ghost written). Due in no small part to the elevation of Wellington to national hero these works tend to highlight service in the Peninsula War. The benefit has been to draw attention to the at times dire supply situation soldiers experienced in this conflict.

Descriptions of tattered uniforms and of going without food for days highlight failures in logistics that the hard data of Commissariat ledgers could not. The system's greatest failings was its blindness to the plight of soldiers. This impacted operations and efficiencies. The problem, of course, is that in the clamor for experiences of the Peninsular War other theatres and regions are over looked. The fact is that without the memoirists and diarists the experience elsewhere is less clear. It seems inconceivable, however, that there were not times of shortage elsewhere and that soldiers lived off the land. Just how many soldiers needed that 'killing' to get by each day is impossible to estimate.

Bibliography

National Army Museum

NAM 5903/127/6, letters of William Grenville-Eliot, R.A.

NAM 6112/78, Wetherall Papers, Inspection Returns and Correspondence of Major General F. A. Wetherall.

NAM 6112/689, Field Equipment Return for the 1st Battalion 88th Foot, 9th June 1815.

NAM 6309/138, Various Letters from the Duke of Northumberland.

NAM 6801/43, Letter from Irish Militia Surgeons to the Duke of York Expressing Concerns about Pay, c1804.

NAM 6807/71, Notebook of Lieutenant John Ford 1808 – 12.

NAM 6807/163, Bingham Letters.

NAM 6807/221, Books of Commissary General N. Jackson, c1814.

NAM 6807/370/29, Orders For Regimental Hospitals, 1804.

NAM 6807/370/43, Notices Announcing a Curfew in Cork, 4th September 1795.

NAM 6807/370/44, John Travers to Lord Lismore, Cork, 4th September 1795.

NAM 7008/11, Dent Letters.

NAM 7211/58/1, Barrack Office to Officer Commanding in Barracks at Norwich, 20th September 1797.

NAM 7505/10, J. R. Meade, 'The Subaltern's Elegy' (Spain, 1st July 1813).

NAM 7508/24, Notebook of W. Morris, Conductor of Stores, 1812.

NAM 7508/55/2, Particular Account Number 2. Being for Monies Paid and Advanced by Matthew Atkinson, Agent General.

NAM 7512/124, Supplies to the Divisions of the Centre Army Corps in the Peninsula, December 1813.

NAM 7902/36, Account Book of Assistant Commissary General George

Grellier.
NAM 7912/21, Anon, *Life in the 38th Foot.*
NAM 8301/102, Memoirs of Captain Peter Jennings.

Public Records Office

PRO ADM 102/1, Hospital Ship Musters.

PRO ADM 201/20, Discharges, Pay, Pensions and Allowances (Royal Marines).

PRO PC 1/3643-4087, Privy Council Miscellaneous Unbound Papers, February 1805 to March 1816.

PRO T 1/1061, Instructions to His Majesty's Deputy Commissary of Accounts.

PRO WO 1/228-248, War Department in Letters and Papers, June 1808 to March 1811.

PRO WO 12/1522 to WO 12/1530, Royal Wagon Train 1799 – 1817.

PRO WO 12/12017, Royal Wagon Train Foreign Corps, 1816.

PRO WO 17/2813, Monthly returns of the British army at home and abroad, Jan 1803 - Aug 1805, with at front, scale of age and standards for recruits, 1802-1808, and scale of bounty, 1802-1823.

PRO WO 17/2814, Monthly Returns of the Army at Home and Abroad.

PRO WO 17/53-54, Wagon Train 1799–1812.

PRO WO 25/254, Payments by the Commissariat 1812 – 30.

PRO WO 25/3995, Register of Annual Bounty Paid to Deceased Officers Widows.

PRO WO 27/92, Office of Commander in Chief and War Office: Adjutant General and Army Council Inspections.

PRO WO 28/14, Letters from Quarter Master General's Department, 1816 January to June.

PRO WO 30/116, Report on the Coast of Dorsetshire, 1798.

PRO WO 30/141, Proposals for Rendering the Body of the People

Instrumental in the General Defence, saving their property, and distressing the enemy, by removing the means of subsistence, from threatened parts of the country. Published by authority.
PRO WO 37/10/26, Papers Relating to Provision of Portable Forges.
PRO WO 43/296, Amalgamation of Boards of General Officers with Inspectorate of Clothing to form the Consolidated Board
PRO WO 55/635, Miscellaneous Orders to Commissariat.
PRO WO 55/1314, Letters to Board of Ordnance from Adjutant General, February 1807 to July 1809.
PRO WO 55/1369, Adjutant General's Confidential Letters (Outward), September 1810 to February 1816.
PRO WO 55/1548/17, Regulations for each county, in case of Invasion.
PRO WO 61/25, Commissariat Department 1816 – 17.
PRO WO 63/40-49, Letters to Commissariat Officers 1803 – 1815.
PRO WO 63/88-91, Entry Book of Letters Received at Commissariat Headquarters, Dublin, 1805 – 1812.
PRO WO 43/366, Wound gratuity refused to army surgeon Robert Shakelton.
PRO WO 245/134, W. Horton to Deputy Treasurer of Chelsea Hospital, Glasgow, 1816.
PRO WO 377/2, Various Papers, 1809 upon the System of Clothing and Off Reckonings for the Army.

Wiltshire and Swindon Records Office

WSRO A1/752/19, Return of the Qualifications of Deputy Lieutenants and Commissioned Officers [of Wiltshire Militia], 29th January 1796.
WSRO B18/100/7, Salisbury Division, Justices Minute Books, January 1808 to January 1809.
WSRO 632/134, Certificate of Sergeant R. Edwards, Outpatient of Chelsea Hospital, 1834.
WSRO 1719/30, Wiltshire Lieutenancy Papers Dealing with the Parish

[of Box's] Preparation to Raise a Volunteer Force to Meet the Anticipated French Invasion, schedules 1 to 9.

Salisbury Journal 1790 – 1820

Published Sources

Army List, 1790 - 1818 (London, War Office).

Eighth Report of Military Enquiry (London, Office of the Secretary at War, 1809).

Letter from Barrak [sic] *Master General to Barrak Masters* (Barracks Office, 1797).

Statistical Report on the Sickness Mortality and Invaliding Among the Troops of the West Indies (London, HMSO, 1838).

Anon, *A Treatise on Military Finance* (Whitehall, Egerton, 1796).

A. Brett-James (ed), *Edward Costello: The Peninsular and Waterloo Campaigns* (London, Longmans, 1967).

R. N. Buckley (ed), *The Napoleonic War Journal of Captain Thomas Henry Browne 1807 - 1816* (London, Army Records Society, 1987).

S. A. C. Cassels (ed), *Peninsula Portrait 1811 - 1814: The Letters of Captain William Bragge 3rd (Kings Own) Dragoons* (London, OUP, 1963).

T. Chevalier, *A Treatise on Gunshot Wounds* (London, Bagster, 1806).

C. Chilcott, 'English counties and defensive planning, 1803 to 1805', in *Bulletin of the Military Historical Society*, vol. 54, no.215, February 2004, pp.149-154.

- 'The Royal Wagon Train (notes and documents)', in *JSAHR*, volume 82, number 330, Summer 2004, pp.175-177.

M. Glover (ed), *A Gentleman Volunteer: The Letters of George Hennell From the Peninsular War 1812-13* (London, Heinemann, 1979).

W. Grattan, *Adventures with the Connaught Rangers, 1809 - 1814* (London, Greenhill, 1989).

J. Green, *The Vicissitudes of a Soldier's Life* (Cambridge, Ken Trotman, 1996).

L. C. Gurwood (ed), *Despatches and General Orders of the Duke of Wellington* (London, Murray, 1841).

E. Hathaway (ed), *A Dorset Rifleman: The Recollections of Benjamin Harris* (Swanage, Shinglepicker, 1995).

P. Hayward (ed), *Surgeon Henry's Trifles: Events of a Military Life* (London, Chatto & Windus, 1970).

C. Hibbert (ed), *The Wheatley Diary* (London 1964)

- *A Soldier of the 71st* (London, Leo Cooper, 1976).

G. Larpent (ed), *The Private Journal of F S Larpent: Judge Advocate General of British Forces in the Peninsula*, 3 volumes, (London, Richard Bentley, 1853).

J. H. Leslie, *The Dickson Manuscripts,* 4 volumes (Woolwich, 1905)

B. H. Liddell – Hart (ed), *The Letters of Private Wheeler 1809 - 1828* (London, Michael Joseph, 1951).

J. MacDonald, *Instructions for the Conduct of Infantry in Actual Service* (London, Egerton, 1807).

Lieutenant Colonel J. H. Plumridge, *Hospital Ships and Ambulance Trains* (London, Seeley, 1975).

A. L. F. Schauman, *On the Road with Wellington* (London, William Heinemann, 1924).

W. Surtees, *Twenty Five Years in the Rifle Brigade* (London, Greenhill, 1996).

W. Tomkinson, *The Diary of a Cavalry Officer 1809 - 1815* (Staplehurst, Spellmont, 1999).

M. Trustram, *Women of the Regiment: Marriage and the Victorian Army* (Cambridge, CUP, 1984).

L. T. Wilson, *An Enquiry into the state of the Forces of the British Empire* (London, 1804)

INDEX OF TABLES

1. Commissariat accounting categories Page 29
2. Schedule of Commissariat returns Page 32
3. The global deployment of the Commissariat, December 1816 Page 36
4. Commissariat stores and accounts departments, December 1816 Page 37
5. Availability of supplies in the center army corps, December 1813 Page 40
6. Weapon deficiencies amongst three units deployed in Britain, 1808 Page 56
7. Artillery allocated to coastal defense in the county of Dorset, 1798 Page 60
8. An inventory of furniture and utensils in a barracks, c1797 Page 73
9. Active troops in the Royal Wagon Train 1799 – 1817 Page 83
10. Annual pensions received by widows, c1796 Page 101
11. Ahaplains serving in overseas garrisons, 1816 – 20 Page 122
12. Preparations for invasion, schedules one to nine Page 129

INDEX

Regiments of the British army

10th Light Dragoons, 63
20th Light Dragoons, 56, 57
22nd Light Dragoons, 63
23rd Regiment of Foot, 108
25th Light Dragoons, 97
28th Regiment of Foot, 115
3rd Dragoons, 47
4th Dragoons, 56, 67, 69, 88
4th Queen's Own Dragoons, 65
51st Regiment of Foot, 56
68th Regiment of Foot, 114
71st Regiment of Foot, 43
7th Infantry Division, 45
80th Regiment of Foot, 99
88th Connaught Rangers, 70
88th Regiment of Foot, 44
95th Rifles, 43

A

Act of Union, 1800, 79, 84
Adjutant-General, 22, 56, 69, 113, 120
Admittance to hospital, 112
Advance into France, 48
Africa, 5, 36, 122
Africa, exports of arms to, 55
African colonies, 7
Agriculture, 9, 51
Alcohol, 16, 39, 40, 74
Alcohol, trading of, 46
Amiens, Peace of 1802, 84, 87
Anglican faith, 116, 117, 119
Anti-French propaganda, 131
Armed escort of cooking implements, 44

Army of Occupation, 86, 92
Arthurs, Philip Private, 117
Artillery, 19, 21, 22, 31, 35, 60, 61, 62, 78, 88, 89, 91
Artillery, lack of horses, 25
Asia, campaigns in, 5
Assistant Commissary Generals, 39
Asturias, 25
Austria, 6, 20
Austrian army, 6

B

Badajoz, 70
Baird, Sir David, 34, 35
Bank of England, 14
Barley, 46, 129
Barrack Master General, 52, 69
Barracks, 16, 51, 52, 54, 69, 70, 72, 73, 84, 91, 93, 96, 100, 153
Belem, Spain, 47, 85
Bill of Rights, 1689, 13
Biscuit, 39, 41, 42
Blankets, 74
Board of Ordnance, 24
Boards of General Officers', 64
Bonaparte, Napoleon, 5, 6, 7, 14, 18, 58, 91, 126
Bookbinder, 38
Boyne, Battle of the 1690, 11
Branding irons, 27
Bread, 28, 39, 41, 47, 130, 135, 136, 141
Bread wagons, 92
Bread, baking of, 42
Bread, storage of, 28
British army, 5, 6, 7, 11, 13, 56, 60, 138
British army in Spain, 80
British army, arrival, 24

British Empire, 7, 9, 36, 121
British foreign policy, 20, 62
Buenos Aires, expedition 1806, 20
Burrard, General, 88

C

Cadavers, price of, 107
Cadiz, Spain, 63
Camping equipment, 24
Camping equipment, sell of, 27
Canada, 102
Canadian garrison, 59, 60
Canterbury, 84, 85, 86
Caribbean, 7, 8, 36, 122
Cartwright, Major General, 65, 88
Castelreagh, Robert Stuart Viscount, 88
Catholic churches, 121
Catholicism in the seventeenth century, 11
Catholics, 16, 116, 117, 121, 128
Cato Street Conspiracy, 1820, 57
Cattle, sell of, 27
Cavalry, 17, 21, 22, 31, 32, 45, 58, 60, 65, 66, 69, 83, 87, 88, 89, 90, 91, 96, 102, 138, 139
Cavalry ration, 46
Cavan Militia, 68
Celebration of victories, 51
Chaplain General's Department, 116
Chaplains, 116, 118, 119, 120, 122
Chaplains in Honduras, 121
Chaplains in the militia, 118
Chaplains on campaign, 119
Chaplains outside of Europe, 121, 122
Chaplains, rates of pay, 123
Chaplains, recruitment of, 120
Charles II, 12, 24

Cheese, 47
Chelsea Hospital, 100, 102
Cheques, 30
Chevalier, Thomas Surgeon to the Prince of Wales, 103, 109, 110
Children, 96, 97, 98, 99, 100, 102
Churchill, John Duke of Marlborough, 13
Civil disorder, 57, 58, *126*
Civil disorder, role of army in, 7, 17
Civil service, 8, 14
Clothing Board, 52, 64
Coastal areas, 51
Coastal defenses of Dorset, 60, 61
Cold stores, 28
Colonial garrisons, 59
Colonialism, 7
Commander-in-Chief, 21
Commissariat, 19, 24, 32, 37, 39, 47, 48, 52, 72, 81, 91, 113, 135
Commissariat administrative reforms, 31
Commissariat coopers, 28
Commissariat depots, 25, 26, 27
Commissariat doctrine, 46
Commissariat efficiency, 26
Commissariat foreign personnel, 39
Commissariat in Bermuda, 38
Commissariat in Britain, 38
Commissariat in Calais, 38
Commissariat in Canada, 38
Commissariat in Canada, 38
Commissariat in France, 38
Commissariat in Heligoland, 28
Commissariat in Honduras, 39
Commissariat in Ireland, 26
Commissariat in Malta, 28, 38
Commissariat in Mauritius, 38
Commissariat in Mediterranean, 38
Commissariat in New South Wales, 28, 38

Commissariat in Nova Scotia, 38
Commissariat in Portugal, 38
Commissariat in Sicily, 28
Commissariat in Sicily, 28
Commissariat in Windward and Leeward Islands, 38
Commissariat ledgers, 32, 46
Commissariat Ledgers, 32
Commissariat purchasing agents, 46
Commissariat reports, 31
Commissariat returns, 33, 55
Commissariat stores, 27, 28
Commissariat uniform, 24
Commissariat, strategic planning, 25
Commissary General, 24, 25, 49, 68, 75, 77, 94, 113, 148
Commissary Hagan, disciplinary action against, 31
Committee for Public Accounts, 26
Consolidated Board of General Officers, 64
Contractors, 53, 54, 55, 57, 66, 75, 79, 134
Convalescing personnel, 111, 114
Cooking implements, 44, 72
Cooking implements, transport of, 44
Cork, 16, 35
Corps of Royal Waggoners, 79
Corruption, 30
Costello, Edward Rifleman 95th Rifles, 43
Cromwell, Oliver, 10
Croydon, 84, 86, 93
Currency, 28

D

Danish vessels, 55
Defense of the Realm Act, 127
Deployment of army to Spain, 25
Depot troops of the Royal Wagon Train, 84, 86, 87
Depots, 24, 25, 26
Deputy Adjutant General, 22
Detachments of the Royal Wagon Train, 85, 86
Disbanding Act, 1699, 13
Disorder, *139*, 141
Disorder, involvement of sailors, 15
Disorder, involvement of soldiers in, 14, 16, 17, 40, 70, 72, 100
Disorder, role of the army in, 17
Dissenters, 116
Divine right, 13
Dorset, 60, 153
Dragoons, 44
Draught animals, 33, 87, 130
Dublin, 49
Duke of Monmouth, 11
Duke of York, 21, 99, 105
Dundas, David, 21

E

East India Company, 37
Edwards, Robert Sergeant, 102
Egypt, 63, 65
Eighteenth century Britain, 6, 8, 14
Engineers, 19, 22, 31
English Civil War, 10
Explorers, *15*

F

Falmouth, 35
Families, 95, 96, 97, 98
Fencibles, 19
Fiscal-military state, 8, 9
Flanders, 74, 85
Flanders campaign, 6, 62, 79
Flour, 129, 130, 134, 135, 141
Flour in Lisbon, 42
Flour, production of, 42
Fodder, 39

Fodder, storage of, 28
Followers of the army, 97
Food riots, 57
Footwear, 65
Forage, 31, 45, 46, 54
Forage wagons, 87, 92
Forage, improper storage of, 28
Forage, storage of, 45
Forage, supply of, 24
Foraging parties, 48
Foreign Office, 19
Foreign postings and families, 96, 97
France, 11, 20, 92, 132, 138, 139
Fraud, 30, 31, 33, 102
French actions in Spain, 47
French Army, 6, 7, 18
French navy, 58
French Revolution, 6, 8, 14, 17

G

Glorious Revolution, 11
Grain, 130
Grain imports, 41
Grattan, W. Lieutenant, 70
Greatcoats, 67
Grenville, William, 18
Gross National Product, 51
Guerrillas, 48, 63
Gunshot wounds, 109

H

Hamilton, Digby Colonel, 84, 88
Harwich, 71, 111
Hay, 46, 129, 134, 136
Hay, storage of, 28
Height requirement, 90
Henry Herbert, Earl of Caernarvon, 128
Home Office, 19, 21

Honduras, 122
Horse Guards, 21, 22, 104
Horse transports, 89
Horses, 33, 45, 66, 79, 83, 87, 89, 90, 91, 92, 129, 136, 137
Horses, purchase of, 25, 88
Horses, sell of, 27
Horses, transport of, 88
Horses, unsuitable of combat, 88
Hospital admission, 113
Hospital regulations, 113
Hospital sentinels, 113
Hospital ships, 111
Hospital Ships, 111
Hospital stores, 109
Hospital transfers, 110
Hospital uniform, 113
Hospitals, 8, 104, 106, 107, 109, 110, 111, 112, 113, 114, 115, 121
Hospitals, field, 108
Hospitals, regimental, 112
Howell, Private 71st Regiment of Foot, 43
Hythe, 86, 93

I

Iinfantry, 90
Imperial expansion, 15
Industrialists, 9
Infantry, 22, 34, 60
Infrastructure, 78
Inns, use of, 71, 72, 96
Inoculation, 103
Invasion depots, 134
Invasion planning schedules, 128, 129, 130, 153
Invasion, destruction of equipment, 131
Invasion, evacuation, 131, 136, 137
Invasion, importance of livestock,

131, 133
Invasion, rights of private ownership, 132
Invasion, role of magistrates, 134, 140, 141
Invasion, role of the Commissariat, 133
Invasion, threat of, 58, 61, 126, 127, 128, 129, 130, 131, 132, 133, 136, 138, 140, 141, 153
Invasion, use of villages, 134
Ireland, 11, 26, 31, 68, 91, 141
Ireland, embarkation in, 98
Ireland, recruits from, 16
Irish churches, 121
Irish Rebellion of 1798, 6, 17, 58, 59
Irish Wagon Train, 84
Irvine, William Surgeon, 105
Isle of Wight, 86, 93

J

Jamaica, 103, 112, 123
James II, 11, 12
Jersey, 117

L

Larpent, Judge Advocate, 43, 47
Ledgers, 81, 132
Ledgers, transport of, 33
Leira, 85
Lisbon, 114
Lisbon, Portugal, 85
London, 58, 104, 107
Longford, Ireland, 43
Looters, 108
Looting of wounded, 107
Lord Lieutenant of Hampshire, 126
Lords Lieutenant, 127, 128, 136, 141
Luddites, 17, 57

M

Magistrates, 78, 79
Mail service, 22
March of the Blanketeers, 1817, 57
Maritime destiny, *15*
Marriage, 96
Master General of the Ordnance, 19, 23
Meat, 39, 41, 44
Medical Board, 103, 113
Medical Department, 104
Medical students, 106
Medway, Battle of 1667, *15*
Menagerie of General Cole, 45
Methodists, 116, 117
Military discipline, 16
Militia, 19, 21, 32, 90, 102, 105, 117, 118, 127, 137, 138
Mining, 51
Ministry of Talents, 18
Mobile forges, 33
Monck, George General, 10
Monroe doctrine, 20
Moore, Sir John General, 25, 89
Morris, W. Conductor of Stores, 34
Mules, 33, 45, 46, 81, 90, 110
Mules, purchase of, 25
Mules, sell of, 27
Muleteers, 30, 39, 80, 81, 83
Munitions, 53, 55, 56, 59, 61, 62, 63, 69, 140
Munitions, supply of, 23
Muskets, 63
Mutiny, 16
Mutiny, Nore and Spithead, 17

N

Napoleonic Wars, 8, 75, 96, 102
National debt, 14
New Model Army, 10

New South Wales, 36, 122
North American colonies, 6
Norwich garrison, 54

O

Oats, 46, 129, 134, 136
Ordnance Board, 19, 21, 22, 23, 53, 55
Oxen, 33, 79, 80, 90, 129

P

Parliament, 13, 14, 18, 19, 21
Parliamentary enquiry, 54
Paymasters, 81
Peninsula War, 6, 39
Pensions, 100, 101, 102, 103, 153
Perceival, Spencer, 57
Peterloo Massacre, 58
Pikes, 139
Pioneers, 138
Pitt, William, 18, 72
Portsmouth, 86
Portugal, 20
Portuguese army, 62
Portuguese harvest, 42
Portuguese law, 53
Portuguese stores, 55, 63
Portuguese wives, 97, 98
Prime Minister, 18, 72
Prisoners of war, 105
Promissory notes, 25, 30
Proposals for Rendering the Body of the People Instrumental in the General Defence, 126
Protestants, 16, 16, 117, 120, 121, 128
Provost Marshal, 53
Prussian army, 6, 104

Q

Quakers, 128
Quarter Master General, 24, 52, 74, 123, 149
Quartermaster General, 22
Quiberon, Battle of 1759, *15*

R

Recruiting sergeants, 16
Recruitment, 90, 95
Recruitment bounty, 90
Reforms, 22
Regimental schools, 121
Regulations, 97
Religion, 115, 116, 118
Religious conversion, 118
Religious sermons, 120
Removal of stores, 31
Reports of Military Enquiry, 26
Revolutionary War, outbreak of, 17
Rifle Brigade, 69, 118
Rio Mayor, 85
Role of the monarch, 18
Royal Artillery, 33, 59, 90, 96
Royal Artillery in Malta, 67
Royal Artillery in Spain, 61
Royal Artillery, organization of, 22
Royal Colleges of Surgeons, 104, 110
Royal influence, 18
Royal Navy, 15, 17, *23*, 51, *55*, *62*, *63*, 75, 89, *101*, *103*, 111, *132*
Royal power, 13
Royal Wagon Corps, 79
Royal Wagon Train, 79, 80, 81, 82, 83, 84, 85, 86, 87, 88, 90, 91, 92, 93, 153
Royal Wagon Train artificers, 82
Royal Wagon Train deployment to

Spain, 85
Royal Wagon Train enlistment, 90
Royal Wagon Train foreign personnel, 91, 92
Royal Wagon Train headquarters, 84
Royal Wagon Train in 1816, 92
Royal Wagon Train in Britain, 86, 87
Royal Wagon Train in Hanover, 86
Royal Wagon Train organization, 85
Royal Wagon Train quarter masters, 86
Royal Wagon Train returns, 87
Royal Wagon Train, demobilization of, 91, 92
Royal Wagon Train, organization, 83
Russia, 6
Russian army, 6
Russian vessels, 55

S

Sailors, 17, 51, 103
Sailors, isolation aboard ship, 15
Salamanca, Battle of 1812, 108
Salisbury, 11
Sandhurst, 93
Schools, 22, 99, 100
Scotland, 11
Scots Greys, 17
Scottish regiments, 12
Secretary of State for War and the Colonies, 18, 19, 21, 35, 101
Sedgemoor, Battle of 1685, 11
Seditious Meeting Act, 1795, 120
Shakelton, Robert Surgeon, 105
Sheep, 45, 129, 136
Sheep, South Downs, 136
Sieges, 61, 62, 67
Slavery, 8
Snuff, 53
South America, 20

Spa Fields, 57
Spain, 17, 20, 89, 118
Spain, arrival of British army, 34
Spanish army, 62, 63
Spanish roads, 34
Spanish wives, 98
Spencer, General, 88
Standing army, 12, 15
State funded education, 100
Store Master General, 24
Storekeepers, 25
Stores department, 37
Stuart, House of, 10, 11
Subaltern's Elergy, 43
Sunday Observance Act, 1781, 120
Sunday service, 117, 119, 120
Surgeon, 82, 103
Surgeons, 101, 103, 104, 105, 110
Surgeons, compensation for injuries, 105
Surtees, William Quarter Master, 118
Swedish vessels, 55

T

Tagus, River, 63
Talavera, Battle of 1809, 42, 109
Tangier garrison, 12
Tangiers garrison, 99
Taxation, 8, 9, 14
Tents, 70
Tobacco, 53
Torbay, landing of William III, 11
Treasury, 19, 24
Trotter, John, 54
Tudor Navy, 111
Turnball, Forbes & Co, exporter, 55

U

Unburied corpses, 108
Uniform, 52, 63, 65, 67, 68, 69

Uniform in the field, 64
Uniform of surgeons, 105
Uniform regulations, 64, 65, 67, 68
Uniform, damage of, 27
Uniform, provision of, 64
Uniforms, 33
United States of America, 5, 20
Use of civilian homes, 70, 71

V

Veterinary Surgeons, 82
Volunteers, 19, 21, 90, 118, 128, 139, 140, 141

W

Wagons, 87, 88, 129
Wagons during invasion, 130, 131, 134, 137
Wagons, allocation of, 33, 81, 84, 87, 107
Wagons, maintenance of, 81, 82
Wagons, movement of, 78
Wagons, payment of civilian drivers, 79
Wagons, Spanish and Portuguese, 80
Walcheren Expedition 1809, 20, 71, 106
War of 1812, 5, 57
Ward sergeants, 113
Wars of the Spanish Succession, 14
Waterloo, Battle of 1815, 5, 18, 108, 120
Welfare, 95
Wellington, Arthur Wellesley, Duke of, 6, 41, 43, 55, 63, 64, 66, 79, 80, 88, 89, 95, 97, 107, 109, 114, 144
West Indies,, 16, 112
Widows, 97, 98, 101, 153

William III, 11, 12, 13, 14, 18
Wiltshire, 79
Wiltshire Militia, 102, 128
Windham, William, 101
Wives, 96, 97, 98
Wives and looting, 108
Woodward, B. Major, 68
Woolwich Arsenal, London, 55
Wounded, 81, 106, 107, 108, 109, 110, 111, 112, 130
Wounded, transport of, 34, 107
Wounded, transportation of, 110
Wounds, treatment of, 110

Y

Yeast, 41, 135
Yeast, recipe for, 135
York, Duke of, 21, 22, 99, 100

Z

Zulu Wars, 108

Chris Chilcott

Printed in Great Britain
by Amazon